Witches & Shamans (From Voodoo to Wicca)

The Complete History of Witchcraft and Magic in America

Ivy Holloway

I dedicate this book to my beautiful sister Sue and her wonderful husband Paul. Their dedication to each other is inspiring and their love and support of family are a great example for all. Thank you for being there for me through all of my ups and downs and for always encouraging me to keep trying.

Table of Contents

Introduction

Witchcraft has fascinated people since ancient times, and it still does. A part of human nature needs to believe in some supernatural level of existence. The universe and existence are full of mysteries that can't be comprehended through reason alone. Something more is needed to explain what happens and also to control it. Throughout history, each society has assigned a particular place to witchcraft. For some, it was a religious or spiritual practice; for others, witchcraft was perceived as a malevolent practice, and those accused of practicing it were persecuted and excluded. Witchcraft has been used as a means of power, either to subdue or to resist.

This book aims to explain the development of witchcraft through the ages in America, describing and analyzing the changes and continuities. Also explored is the blending of different cultures as a consequence of political and social processes that took place in the continent before the arrival of the European settlers until the present. We shall start by learning about the religious practices carried out by the indigenous people—such as shamanism, among others—that can be conceived as mysticism and witchcraft. At the end of the 15th century, European colonization began, and with the settlers, new beliefs and practices were introduced to America, bringing different impacts on the local communities. The settlers didn't only bring the traditional European religions

(Catholicism and Puritanism) but also pagan practices such as Wicca.

Later, colonialist powers introduced African enslaved people, an economic exploitation system that persisted for many years after the independence processes and the institution of American countries as autonomous states. African people carried their own mystical and witchcraft-like practices, such as voodoo, and clashed or merged with the other local beliefs and practices.

Throughout the centuries, all these cultural legacies expressed through mystical practices have combined. Today, they still persist as a mixture amongst the different cultures, retrieving components from some of them to create new ways to experience spirituality that lead us into the New Age movement, a new era of religions perhaps. Believing in magic or witchcraft was, for a long time, associated with lower levels of development in society. In the linear evolution of humankind through history, magical thinking was used by ancient social groups to find answers to everything in nature and the existential questions of life. With the advance of science and rational thinking, this magical hypothesis was replaced with theories and sophisticated empirical demonstrations. At present, that posture is challenged by the coexistence of both systems of ideas.

Spiritual practices combine a conglomerate of beliefs, deities, and cosmogony that can be or not be organized systematically. The main purpose of the book is to describe witchcraft and the many practices that fall under this umbrella term, with the particular features adopted by societies throughout the American people's history. It is difficult to talk about witchcraft as one uniform body of practices, and the concept is charged with many meanings, some coming from common sense and some others from prejudices.

Before exploring witchcraft for different cultures at different moments of history in America, I shall state what definition of witchcraft frames this book. Even though Chapter 1 provides an extensive explanation of different ways to define and explain witchcraft and magic, let's say for the moment that witchcraft implies believing in the existence of supernatural powers strong enough to alter material reality and human beings' lives. These supernatural powers are venerated, feared, pacified, or irritated depending on the believers' attitudes and behaviors and can be effectively interpreted and manipulated by certain people through specific esoteric practices (Breslaw, 2000).

It must be noted that the concept of "witchcraft" as a way to typify a social practice, regardless of its relationship with paranormal phenomena, is influenced by modern Western thinking. In other words, American Native people, European pagans, and African enslaved people didn't make the distinction between witchcraft, magic, sorcery, and all the other terms that have been coined to explain and name those practices. Shamanism, Wicca, or Voodoo were simply practiced. Many interpretations and assumptions are swayed by the observer's mindset. Nonetheless, I have endeavored to describe rituals and practices objectively and provide the social and historical background explanation so you can relocate the practices in the original context of production.

This manuscript attempts to draw a general picture of what witchcraft and other mystical practices (shamanism, voodoo, Wicca, and others) are and what they mean or meant in the context of some particular American societies. It would be difficult to cover in detail every American community or delve deep into each moment of the historical evolution. Therefore, I have selected some of the most significant social groups and milestones in the history of witchcraft on the continent. The analysis of each practice in every social group will include the statements and system of beliefs as well as the practices and behaviors performed by the believers and how witchcraft and mysticism, or the fear of it, worked in those particular societies.

Witchcraft and its effects can be a matter of controversy. The book aims to leave those controversies aside and focus on describing witchcraft and other mystical practices in the context where they are created and the social role they play. I intend to provide descriptions and explanations to help the reader put into context practices that, from a contemporary foreign perspective, can acquire a very different meaning from that assigned by the people who carried them out.

This book doesn't aim to convince any reader to follow or adhere to any of the practices I describe here. The reader has the great challenge of leaving any bias aside to learn about different religious and spiritual practices and beliefs that are built through social interaction as a result of long-lasting complex social processes. We aren't requested to convert nor to judge.

These pages bring you an invitation to discover other worldviews that will enrich our own and develop tolerance and acceptance of different cultures. It isn't such an easy exercise but it is necessary. We live in a global heterogeneous society, and radically different worldviews coexist. The more open-minded and tolerant we are, the better our understanding and respect for human and cultural diversity.

Spirituality is a dimension of our human nature and plays a key role in social life. Contemporary societies seem to be ruled by materialistic, productive, and rational patterns. While the traditional idea of religion might seem to be increasingly questioned, people continue to search for new ways to transcend objective reality and connect to deeper and genuine expressions of spiritual life. While some scholars speak about the disenchantment of the world, new currents like the New Age Movement emerge to prove that mysticism and spirituality might merge, change, and evolve but never disappear; it is just a new page in history being written.

Chapter 1: Witches and Shamans— What Are They?

Each society has a particular definition of witchcraft. The concept can appeal to different types of practices that have a lot in common but, at the same time, have many specific features. Magic, sorcery, voodoo, *brujería*, and many others are all some kind of witchcraft. It can be assumed that the main general characteristic is the belief in the existence of supernatural powers that can influence people's lives, and it is possible to control and be deliberately used for certain purposes.

The other common factor between witchcraft practices: The possibility to communicate and deal with supernatural powers is restricted to some people with a natural ability to perform as mediators between both worlds or those who acquire it through special training. The witch, the sorcerer, the wizard, and the shaman are some of them. Therefore, it is necessary to know the community where the type of witchcraft originated and practiced and divide the community of believers into those who demand the use of those powers and the ones capable of using them.

Finally, there is a major difference in the role each type of witchcraft played in the society where it originated, and many times, it reflected social asymmetries or political unrest. From ancient times, the knowledge of natural processes gave some people special powers. In many societies, those people were the priestly class. They ordered when to seed, when to harvest, when to go to war, and could predict weather phenomena. People believed those were supernatural powers. In highly developed societies, those beliefs and practices evolved as traditional religions, with standardized rituals, hierarchical structures, and an organized system of beliefs. In less complex societies, the power that came with knowledge was concentrated in a man or a woman who might also have political power but played other significant roles within society.

In general, witchcraft was developed by the lower social classes to attend to their primary needs. Witchcraft didn't only exist in primitive, simple societies. Instead, all societies develop some sort of witchcraft practices and beliefs. Modern Western societies were populated with folk witches, wizards, and sorcerers. Contemporary societies still preserve ancient practices that involve magic. People believed in supernatural powers as a way to resist a system that excluded them. Folk healers and witches, then, played an important role in keeping social order and comforting people in times of scarcity or crisis.

Witchcraft and Magic Through History and in Different Cultures

It is common to find witchcraft and magic used as exchangeable terms. They both refer to a system of rites, rituals, and beliefs that provide a way to comprehend the whole world, recognize the different nature of forces that interact to build reality, and enable the practitioners to gain some level of control over them. These people can even reach special levels of consciousness to contact paranormal entities (Bailey, 2006). Life is so full of threats and uncertainties that magic or witchcraft—as traditional religions and other spiritual practices—provides a little bit of hope and a sense of security to people. Witchcraft was a way to find answers, predict the future, protect against evil or bad luck, and heal the ills of the body and the soul (Farrell et al., n.d.), and at the dawn of a new millennium, it hasn't disappeared.

Some approaches have defined witchcraft as a community of people who consider themselves witches or magicians (Farrell et al., n.d.). That means that they share a system of rituals and knowledge and believe in their own ability to control supernatural forces. Yet, what is considered witchcraft and how it fits society has usually been defined by the power centers. At different moments of history, and in particular in America after the arrival of the European conquerors, any religious or spiritual practice was judged from a European perspective and categorized as witchcraft as an attempt to demonize them. This was a way to reduce the power they had over their own communities (Farrell et al., n.d.). In this sense, people weren't believed to perform magic or witchcraft as socially accepted activities but were accused of it. Witchcraft and magic were illegal activities censored and persecuted since they challenged the established power.

In the Americas, many concepts about witchcraft had particular meanings regarding the local communities and the influence of the foreign population they interacted with.

In Latin America, witchcraft accusations fell mostly on women. In Chapter 5, we shall discuss why witch hunts were predominantly carried out on women first in Europe, later in America, and anywhere in the world, even at present. Before the arrival of the Europeans, there were many figures in the native communities associated with different types of witchcraft practices. Most of them played the role of folk healers, wizards, and folk witches, analog figures developed in European medieval societies. Nonetheless, the idea of witches and magicians capable of flying and casting spells can be traced back to ancient Greece in the Western world (Kramer, n.d.).

A contemporary approach to witchcraft retrieves different contributions coming from several new movements such as New Age and Neo-paganism. Others recall modern Western Wicca, which was based on pre-Catholic practices developed by ancient European people like the Celts. In fact, from a Eurocentric perspective rooted in the Christian-Catholic mindset, witchcraft is linked to the term Wicca, which means "wise one" (Farrell et al., n.d.). This conception is charged with a negative connotation since Wicca and other pagan practices were suppressed or reduced as the Catholic church gained power in the continent, and Catholicism became the majority religion due in part to the evolution of social processes and in another part to the result of political procedures that compelled people to converse.

The first version of the witch stands quite close to the one that has remained in the popular imagination. It originated in the western Alps, and it represented the winter and the cold. Originally, she had the mission to punish disobedience and reward good behavior. Later, she was given magical powers she could carry in her own body or in some artifact, which was used to hurt other people (Kramer, n.d.). As time passed by, the figure of the witch represented everything that was wrong within society: evil, old age (therefore infertile), and ugliness. She lived alone, unmarried, isolated, and excluded from the rest. She was feared but also sought after in times of desperation.

In the popular imagination, witchcraft is associated with evil, the dark side of human beings, and nature. Witches, particularly women, are the villains in traditional tales, are usually associated with the devil and other demonic spirits, and use their supernatural power to hurt others. Wizards, on the contrary, are linked to wisdom and have entered the popular culture as those who advise and protect.

This is the general overview of witchcraft that reached America through the first colonialist expeditions that started at the end of the 15th century. In this book, I have divided American history into three main stages: the pre-colonial period, to refer to Native American people's witchcraft and other spiritual practices; the colonial period, which covers the arrival of the European conquerors and the centuries of the colonial domination in the continent, including the introduction of the African enslaved people with their culture and own mystical ideas; and the evolution in the last two centuries, after the independence processes.

The original picture of the witch and the negative conception of witchcraft, added to the use of religion as a means to subjugate the local communities, determined that sometimes some practices disappeared or were taken underground, but some other times, they blended and created new ways to satisfy spiritual needs. However, over 500 years after the European arrival to America, some of the pre-existent practices continue to survive. Other contemporary feminist perspectives link the power of witches with a new women's identity, free and empowered, as a way to oppose the patriarchal society (Hutton, 2017).

It is important to mention that along with witchcraft and magical practices, this book also covers the complete imagination of mystical creatures and deities that usually are part of the system of beliefs. The worldview and the whole system of beliefs of a particular society helps us understand what witchcraft and magic mean to them and why it can be considered either a means of social order or a threat.

Do Witches Exist? Witches, Healers, and Shamans

Within the Western tradition, there is a major division between two types of people with magical or supernatural powers: First, the "worker of the harmful magic," which refers to the evil witch of the fairy tales and urban legends, also known as the "folk witch," and second, the so-called "white witch" or "good witch" who performs different types of services to the community and can also have religious or priestly functions (Clifton, 2019). The latter are also called folk healers, witch doctors, cunning folks, and shamans. All of these terms refer to particular figures, are a product of different social environments, and have special powers and social roles. Even though they originated a long time ago, and those origins reflect pre-capitalist societies, the truth is that they persist in contemporary societies all over the world. However, the following explanations attempt to describe how they emerged and what each of them entails.

The folk witch is a figure created by the popular imagination. The concept originated in rural pre-capitalist societies and can be considered an intuitive, non-rational answer to human beings' deepest fears. The idea of a witch represents evil among human beings. Terrible things have always happened to people, and rational explanations are often not available or not sufficiently convincing. This creature that belongs to the folk narrative realm is capable of performing harmful activities, unfolding misfortune, and is equipped with some magical tools, such as brooms that allow them to fly and dance around trees (Magliocco, 2009). The folk witch is also depicted as an old woman that lives alone, has a black cat, organizes encounters with the devil or other witches, and prepares deadly magic potions in a boiling cauldron. The male equivalent of the folk witch is the sorcerer, a male magician who performs magic to cause harm.

Witches are usually accompanied by the popular image of a gathering to invoke the Devil. Those gatherings are called the witches Sabbath. The concept originated in Europe in the 14th and 15th centuries, and it recalls a ritual where many witches reunited to encounter the Devil and other demons and have ignominious parties. There, the witches sealed a deal with the Devil, rejected the Christian faith, and entailed dark arts practice—malevolent magic (Schoonmaker, 2015). The witches' Sabbath image was introduced into America by the Europeans and acquired different names. The spread of the witches' Sabbath among the population strengthened the demonization of witches or anyone accused of witchcraft.

This idea of a witch didn't exist in those terms in America before the arrival of the Europeans. Nonetheless, Native people did believe in the existence of people with evil supernatural powers and feared them. They were commonly outsiders or figures associated with enemy tribes.

The folk witch as the embodiment of evil was also applied to people rejected by the community. Anyone with misfit behaviors could be accused of witchcraft. It played a significant role in dealing with domestic and internal conflicts within the communities. Hostilities among the neighbors that couldn't be solved—or were neglected—by the institutionalized powers were turned into a witchcraft accusation. This isn't necessarily what triggered witch hunts, as will be explained later. It is a social mechanism of conflict resolution. At present, it continues to exist.

While the folk witch was normally represented as a woman, the "white witch" or the good-magic performer could be either male or female figures, depending on the society. One of those figures was the cunning folks, people with the knowledge or power to heal. The term "cunning folk" was coined by the English tradition ("Cunning Folk and Conjurors: Folk Magic in Colonial Virginia," 2016). In different Western societies, they receive many different names: folk healers, *guaritori*, *donne che aiutano*, *praticos*, *mago* or *maghiarja*, among others (Magliocco, 2009), *machis* ("Machi Francisca Linconao,", 2018), and shamans in American native communities, and "conjurors" for the African and African-American tradition ("Cunning Folk and Conjurors: Folk Magic in Colonial Virginia," 2016). In Europe, the cunning folk were usually associated with women because healing was closely linked to domestic roles. However, they could also be men. For instance, shamans are mostly men.

The cunning folk can be defined as "the healer of the sick, the interpreter of the Unknown, the comforter of the sorrowing, the supernatural avenger of wrong" ("Cunning Folk and Conjurors: Folk Magic in Colonial Virginia," 2016). They offered a service to the community by healing the illnesses of the body and the soul. Their role was important in societies or social groups where people had little access to health care. In European medieval and modern societies, the peasants couldn't afford a physician. Therefore, they resorted to cunning folks. In contemporary non-capitalist societies, cunning folks under many other names continue to play a similar role where science or modern medical care systems aren't developed or out of reach.

Cunning folks were classified into two groups. Some of them were capable of healing due to their knowledge of the curative properties of the local plants (herbs). They were used in many different ways to heal the pains of the body, but also some of the soul: to prepare poultices or make infusions. However, while some plants have medicinal properties, others can be poisonous, and sometimes, the substances can have two opposing effects depending on the use and dose. Cunning folks, then, had the power to use herbs for any purpose the client requested from them.

The other type of cunning folks or cunning healers treated the pains of the spirit more specifically. This was related to more personal powers and not to knowledge. The power was a personal trait of the folk or the healer and was performed through prayers, rituals, magical formulas, and other techniques. While the first type of knowledge (of plants) could be acquired through lectures and training, supernatural personal powers came with the individual. Some traditions concede that it could be transmitted from the cunning folk or healer to other individuals at particular moments of the year and through specific rituals. For instance, it could be through an initiation ritual that had to be carried out at midnight on Christmas Eve (which coincides with the solstice, an important moment for many cultures around the world), or it was also possible that the power could be passed through generations within a family (Magliocco, 2009).

In America, cunning folks adopt different names and assume other more important roles within the community. For instance, the *machis* among the Mapuche people in South America (Chile and Argentina) are female figures with great knowledge of the local herbs to heal bodies and souls but are also the political leaders of the tribes ("Machi Francisca Linconao," 2018).

The shamans are the equivalent of the cunning healer in many communities in America and also in other parts of the world. Nonetheless, there are some important differences between a shaman and a cunning folk. First, the shamans—predominantly men—also play religious and priestly functions and unify civil and religious powers. They are believed to have a supernatural power that is inherited within the family. In some tribes, the shaman's power can be obtained through specific natural fitness (Webb Hodge & Alexander, n.d.).

In some communities, the same person with the power to heal could also cause great damage. Therefore, in those cases, it is difficult to draw a line between what would be considered cunning folk and a sorcerer. There is an American legend that tells the story of a shaman with evil powers, the Tahquitz, a shaman of the tribes that inhabited the West deserts in the United States. These shamans could heal illnesses, make it rain, and bring luck for a good hunt (Clapp & Patencio, n.d.). This type of shaman performed their acts in secret, more like a sorcerer. Shamans, unlike sorcerers (for the bad) and cunning folks (for the good), carried out their rituals in public since they embodied public power. They had to prove that power in front of the eyes of their community.

So far, we can say that witchcraft has been historically conceived as a source of power that can be used to influence the force of nature and achieve certain purposes for the benefit of people. Nonetheless, at the same time, it could also represent something to be afraid of. Witchcraft and magic were simultaneously a means to protect from evil and something to be afraid of. Among the most disadvantaged segments of the population, magic was both the answer to some of their problems and the solution. Through what is called "everyday magic" or "folk magic" ("Cunning Folk and Conjurors: Folk Magic in Colonial Virginia," 2016) and witchcraft, they hoped to ward off evil, bring good fortune, heal illnesses, and bring abundance to their homes. People practiced folk magic on both sides of the Atlantic to protect themselves from harm and pernicious spirits.

Other Magical Practices and Artifacts

When speaking about witchcraft and magic, it is important to notice once more that depending on the society where the practices are located, it would be more accurate to talk about religious or spiritual practices. These terms are a broader umbrella that allows us to include all the beliefs about supernatural or non-material entities that coexist in the world with objective reality and other levels of existence. For instance, we can refer to Hell and Heaven or any other way to refer to life after death or the place where demons and deities live. Supernatural creatures might include gods and goddesses, spirits, fairies, monsters, and ghosts, among many others. The system of beliefs that can entail the spiritual background of a society or social group entails all that and more. The rites, rituals, prayers or written formulas, books, and artifacts.

Witchcraft and magical practices are another way to communicate and interact with that paranormal universe and achieve certain goals. In the previous section, we explored the different figures that appeared throughout time in societies. Now, we shall describe some of those practices and the instruments or accessories that they might entail.

Performing magical practices involves particular formulas. Some are based on herbs and substances to create potions or poultices (like the cunning folks did) to cure illnesses or comfort the soul. Many other formulas are made of combined words. Those are called enchantments, spells, and curses, which are lyrical compositions with a secret connotative meaning that can only be revealed or known by some people (witches and sorcerers, for instance). It is believed that the repetition of certain words (three times a word, as three is a magical number), the rhythm, the sounds, and other ritual elements help people to achieve special levels of consciousness. Therefore, these rhymes predispose the mind to magical phenomena to occur (Waterman, 2017). Spells and chants might have the power to control the forces of nature, twist human fate, or cause changes to matter.

Maleficium is considered one magical practice exclusively used to curse or cause damage. It involves resorting to the Devil or malignant creatures. The *maleficium* was also used to accuse people of witchcraft, regardless of their actions. If something happened in the village or to someone, it was charged on *maleficium* carried out by someone who could be accused of witchcraft. It was used to explain or justify misfortune. In this sense, this practice plays a role of social control and a sort of popular justice in some communities (Blécourt & Davies, 2020). Even though *maleficium* implies resorting to malevolent powers, it could be for a good purpose, for instance, recovering personal properties or finding missing objects.

Another typical magical practice is scrying and divination. One of the greatest concerns of human beings is about the future: What comes next? Therefore, the attempt to know the future and control it or twist it is another relevant practice of witchcraft. There are several techniques to foresee the unknown—the future but also the past and the present. The skills of divination also allow us to see whatever is required. Scrying, in particular, refers to a practice that involves a person that acts like a medium and receives messages through reflective surfaces such as speculas, crystal balls, mirrors, or water (Wigington, 2019). These objects are some of the many that are used to predict the future, for instance, cards, rocks, and elements of nature.

Witchcraft and magical practices entail special speeches and artifacts that are integrated through rituals and rites. In America, some of the artifacts employed in the rituals are linked to animate beings. People attributed inanimate objects to the features of a living being. Statues, altars, pottery, and many others are assigned magical or supernatural characteristics (Walker & Berryman, 2023). In Europe, the use of artifacts is rooted in paganism practices and was later blended with Catholicism by the personification of the sacred figures in statues (the Virgin, Jesus, the saints).

Different materials and objects have also been incorporated into rituals claiming protection or healing. Others are used for good luck. They are called amulets and talismans, and cultures around the world have created hundreds. Amulets are objects believed to have special powers, and talismans need to be charged by a witch or a magician. Talismans are mainly used for protective purposes, and amulets attract good energy and fortune (Gaspar, 2013).

Many types of artifacts employed in rituals have been used by people of the Americas. Pueblo people, a community that lived in the northwest of Mexico, used ashes, projectile points, minerals, and many others as ritual artifacts predominantly to provide themself protection (Walker & Berryman, 2023).

Cunning folks used a great variety of ritual objects, methods, and artifacts, including weapons, to fight against the evil spirits that sickened the body or the soul. They used to build and bury artifacts to protect people or the village from the attack of the evil witch (both figures coexisted without contradiction). Many of those artifacts and technologies are retrieved by contemporary Neo-Pagan witches, who also use altars where the spiritual and the material world can join and interact (Magliocco, 2009). Amulets, talismans, and the use of divination objects are still frequent in modern practices of witchcraft.

Chapter 2: Witchcraft and Magic in America—The Pre-Colonial Period

Europeans arrived in the Americas at the end of the 15th century. First, to Central America, the islands in the Caribbean Sea, and from there, they reached current Mexico and Florida. At the same time, during the 16th century, other expeditions explored the coasts of North America. By land, the Spanish and Portuguese would later reach South America. As the Europeans landed in different spots of the Americas, they ran into the local populations. Since the initial expedition was heading to India, and they didn't know they had reached somewhere else, they gave a mistaken name to all those people. Columbus and the European explorers called them "Indians." Many centuries later, these people have recovered their original names and how they called themselves.

In the following sections of this chapter, we are going to learn about witchcraft and other mystical practices carried out by these people mistakenly called "Indians" by foreigners. To understand the meaning and social roles of those practices, we will learn some relevant aspects of those communities and their culture. We're delving into American witchcraft before the encounter with European mindset and practices.

Mythology and Religious Practices in Native American Cultures

By the time the Europeans arrived in America, millions of people lived on the continent, and they spoke at least 2,000 languages (Digital History, n.d.), each of them representing a different community with a particular culture. They spread from the lands of Alaska to the Southern extreme of Tierra del Fuego island, in present-day Argentina. There were greatly developed empires, such as the Aztecs and the Incas, and some others were sedentary communities with different levels of social organization and technological features to practice agriculture. Many other people lived in small nomadic groups of hunters and gatherers.

Each of them had particular religious and mystical practices that weren't defined as witchcraft by themselves, although many of them also believed in witches and sorcerers as the embodiment of evil.

Now, we shall travel across the continent to meet the people that lived five centuries ago. Many of these cultures survive until the present, but this approach attempts to describe witchcraft and their mystical practices as they were before European intervention.

The history of witchcraft and magical practices has been neglected or hidden by the official records as if it didn't exist. Most of the stories about the practices carried out by the Native American populations reach us through the testimonies written by the colonialists. Some of them were directly heard from the protagonists and written in European languages; others were mediated by interpreters (Boas, 1914). It is possible that parts of their original meaning might be lost, but this is the way we have to learn about them.

North America

Inuit Culture

The Inuit people lived in the northern extreme of the American continent. Over ten thousand years ago, they reached Alaska through the Bering Strait during the last glacial era. They settled in present-day Alaska, surrounding Hudson Bay in current Canada, and the habitable coasts of Greenland.

They lived in a challenging environment, and that developed a worldview deeply interconnected to nature. They believed all that was caused by living creatures of different natures and that everything, animate and inanimate, had a soul. Magic was a part of daily life. If it helped survival, it was accepted. Otherwise, it was cataloged as witchcraft and censored by the community.

The Inuits created ritual objects from different materials such as wood, bones of the animals they hunted, and ivory. When using the bones of animals, the intention was to keep the relationship between the soul of the animal to use it as a helping spirit.

The rituals involved all the members of the community. They were conducted by the *Angakut*, the shaman. He had the ability to communicate with the spirits, heal the body, and foresee the future (Maculotti, 2018). His intervention was recalled to ensure a balance between this world and the Numina, the supernatural world. The *Angakut* was also in charge of fighting against witchcraft.

The *ilisiituk* were the witches among the Inuits. They could be men or women and practiced "black magic" to hurt others. They had the power to steal peoples and animals' souls to manipulate them and make them act in favor of evil purposes. The symptoms of soul loss were paralysis, insanity, and illnesses until the person eventually died. Even though the shamans were healers, it is believed that it was also they who performed acts to steal souls.

The *ilisiituk* created the *tupilak* (plural, tupilat): creatures that took the shape of any living being and were given a soul and the order of causing a type of harm. If the tupilak failed to accomplish its mission, it would go back and kill its creator.

Necromancy was a common practice of witchcraft. It consisted of profaning tombs or altering burial ceremonies. On occasions, the witch would take a part of the enemy's body, say their name and repeat a formula to curse someone. Another method was to take parts of the dead body from a grave and put them among the victim's belongings or in contact with them. This ritual would put the ghost of the dead person against the living victim, and it would search for revenge for offending its burial.

Animals were also used against the chosen victims. After hunting, skins and bones from the hunted animals were placed in the path of the victim, inside the boots or the clothes, while saying the magical words. The ghost of the animal would seek vengeance against the one who had its remains.

Cherokee Shamanism and Magical Formulas

The Cherokee Nation was one of the largest in North America, reaching almost 150,000 people living in the many tribes they had. The Cherokees called themselves Keetoowah or Tsalagi (Encyclopaedia Britannica, 2023) and lived in an extensive area between the Appalachian Mountains—present-time Georgia and eastern Tennessee—and the western region of present-time North and South Carolina.

The Cherokees believed that unnatural death and illnesses were always caused by witchcraft. Death by disease was caused by the intervention of evil spirits, ghosts, and witches who could contact the Shina (Anisgi´na), a sort of demon. Therefore, diseases were treated with magical formulas. Those formulas were orally transmitted through generations until they were collected in several manuscripts. The Cherokees had formulas to treat love issues, make rain fall, cast protective charms, have a successful hunt and fishing, and heal.

Formulas consisted of repeated words. If a shaman's apprentice couldn't remember a formula after hearing it once, he didn't deserve the role. The formulas could only be spelled once or they lost their power. Shamanistic practices were performed secretly and the words were spoken in a low voice to make them intelligible to everybody else. They were spoken while administering beverages of plants with curative properties.

In the Cherokee worldview, plants were human beings' allies to fight against the diseases the animals had created to decrease the race that threatened them. Therefore, each plant had a series of palliative effects that relieved pain.

The herb treatment was applied through a special ritual that included sweat baths in caves, bleeding, and taking a cold bath in streams. Some of those practices were common in many cultures in North America, except the Inuits. The ritual could be carried out in an *â´sĭ*, a small hut made of mud where the person sat alone and naked on the floor. Large heat rocks were placed near the individual and the potions made of the proper plant were poured over the rocks so that the steam would reach and heal the sufferer (Mooney, n.d.).

Plants and magical formulas weren't the only healing practices. It is known that they practiced dance rituals scheduled in accordance with certain moments of the year. One of them is known as the "medicine dance," associated with another similar one called the "medicine boiling dance." The latter was almost as important as the greatest ritual dance, the "green corn dance." These rituals included the use of herbs with magical properties that the participants had to drink for the healing process, including the elimination of evil spirits from the ill body. The Cherokees believed that illness and misfortune were caused by malevolent supernatural forces. The entire community took part in the rituals but was conducted by the local shaman. The shaman offered a service to the community, and for that, he should be paid. The compensation was called *ugista´'ti* (possibly translated as "I take" or "I eat") (Mooney, 1886).

The shaman had great power as he mediated the relationship between two dimensions of reality. For the Cherokee, there were celestial and terrestrial levels of existence settled by the line of the horizon, and there was a constant tension between human beings and the celestial prototypes of everything that exists. The shaman had the knowledge and power to keep the balance between both worlds (Irwing, 1992). While the animals were human beings' antagonists and led them to constant conflict, the plants and herbs were their allies to restore balance and survival.

Navajo People

The ancestors of the Navajo people arrived in the continent between 12,000 and 6,000 B.C.E. Their culture settled and flourished many centuries later in the Colorado Plateau region (Navajo People, n.d.).

The Navajo—or Navaho— call themselves *Diné*, meaning "The People" or "Children of the Holy People," and have their own history of how they emerged on Earth and in America. The Navajo cosmogony states the existence of two types of people: The Holy People and the Earth People. They belong to the second type but were direct descendants of the first group.

Witchcraft was part of the spiritual life of the Navajo people, and it still is. Navajo people have always been terribly scared of ghosts. They believe life doesn't end with death, and people's souls remain near their bodies. That's why they are very careful to avoid settling on cemeteries or places where people have been buried. That's why witchcraft is so closely related to corpses and tombs.

They had different types of practices associated with witchcraft (Palmer, 1974). One of them was witchery. The Navajo people believed in witches who could be either men or women, but they were mostly men. They gathered in isolated places and practiced all types of rituals invoking demons and evil spirits and carrying out prohibited practices. In these reunions, they also performed initiation rituals for new witches.

Navajo believed that witches were very macabre. They profaned graves to obtain corpses either to practice intercourse with them or to eat their flesh. They also used them to prepare all sorts of corpse poison. Witchery consisted mainly of using corpse poison to harm others. They believed that parts of the body held the strength of the person even after they died (Palmer, 1974).

The materials were used to prepare medicine but also to hurt the selected victims. They would take flesh, bones, or the fetus of pregnant women and turn it into powder. They believed that children's corpses were the most effective, especially if they were twin children. The preferred parts of the body to prepare potions and ointments were the bones at the back of the head cut into circles and places where the skin had a pattern of spiral or stripes (like the fingers or the foot's sole).

To cause an effect, the corpse poison was administered by the witch in different ways but the victim had to make contact with it. The witch could pour the potion into the victim's mouth or any other part of the body in their sleep or offer poisoned cigars or food. Sometimes, the witch didn't have the chance to get that close to the victim, so they would approach the victims in the middle of a crowd, in a public event, and blow poisoned powder at their faces.

The most powerful and feared witch was the "skinwalker," "a type of harmful witch who had the ability to turn into, possess, or disguise themselves as an animal" (Carpenter, n.d.). It can be compared to the European folk witch or sorcerer. The Navajo people called it *yee naaldlooshii,* which can be translated as "with it, he goes on all fours."

Navajo skinwalkers were originally folk healers that, at some point, started using their knowledge and power to hurt others. During the day, they had a normal human appearance but turned into animals at night. The skinwalker could be either a male or a female, but they had to go through an initiation rite that implied killing a close member of the family, predominantly a sibling. They could choose the animal they wanted to turn into depending on the skills they required to accomplish a certain task. The skinwalkers could also possess a victim and make them act as they pleased (Carpenter, n.d.). The skinwalkers were blamed for the tragedies that struck the community.

Another type of witchcraft practiced by the Navajo people was sorcery. This required a technique based on words. The sorcerer acted by casting spells on their victims, but they needed to have some personal belongings of the victim. Anything could serve the purpose: hairs, human bowel, saliva, other body fluids, or personal objects. The sorcerer prepared an ointment with certain herbs and spread it on the victim's things as they repeated the magical formulas. This caused illness or death to the victim.

Sorcerers had another procedure to cause damage to the victims. They took something from them—any of the personal objects listed before—and buried it in a grave or under a tree that had been struck by lightning (Palmer, 1974). It only worked if the sorcerer also pronounced the proper spell correctly. These spells were formulas, songs, or saying good prayers backward. If it was impossible to obtain the personal belongings of the victim, the sorcerer could build little dolls or effigies and nail sharp objects to them. This practice resembles another sorcery practice introduced by the African people, voodoo, as we shall learn later.

Besides witchery and sorcery, Navajo people believed in wizardry, another type of witchcraft. Wizards were, almost in all cases, old men, and like witches and sorcerers, had to kill a sibling to obtain and keep their power. Their technique involved the use of plants instead of corpses or personal objects. They prepared potions with plants and herbs and used them to send evil spirits to the victims.

As there were three types of "evil witchcraft practitioners," Navajo people also believed in healing magic. It was practiced by herbalists, shamans, and singers. The shamans provided the diagnosis which considered health as a balance between body, soul, and mind. The shaman was able to discover what caused the imbalance and illness. Then, the shaman started the healing path. It included the assistance of the herbalist and the intervention of the singer, who used magical songs and chanted prayers.

They believed that ghosts caused imbalance and illnesses. If it was a Navajo ghost or witchcraft, they performed a ritual dance to ensure. If it came from a non-Navajo ghost, the ritual attempted to expel the evil from the body of the victim, and the ritual demanded exorcism techniques (Palmer, 1974).

The Aztecs and the Guerra Florida (Flower War)

In the lands of present-day Mexico, a group of people migrated from Aztlan (north of Mexico City) led by the god Huitzilopochtli and settled in the vicinity of lake Texcoco. They were the Aztecs, or the Mexicas as they called themselves. At the beginning of the 14th century, they settled in a region of five interconnected lakes where today stands the city of Mexico. They founded the capital of what became a great empire, the city of Tenochtitlan. They managed religious life, wrote the codices that recorded the rituals and used the astronomical calendar to foresee the future.

There were many other tribes in the region, but the Mexicas and other two allied city-states seized power. They subjugated all the neighboring population and forced them to pay tributes to them. The Aztecs were a warrior empire, and violence was a part of the system employed to maintain their dominance over the other populations.

They had one particular ritual that impressed the first Spanish conquerors led by Hernán Cortez when they first ran into them. It was called the Guerra Florida (Flower War or Flowery War).

The origins of the Flowery Wars were linked to a terrible famine that struck the highlands and the valley where the Mexica lived. Many people died, and others even exchanged their children for food. They believed that the gods were displeased and that was their way to punish them. The priests explained that wars weren't enough, and the gods demanded more blood and sacrifices. Therefore, the people of the allied cities agreed to wage a war that helped the army keep trained and provide fresh and more victims to offer to gods in sacrifices (Milligan, 2023).

According to different sources, the Mexica Emperor Moctezuma I was the first one to order the Flowery War among its allies and over other vassal city-states. The warriors fought each other, and those who were captured were taken to the sacred place where the priests carried out the human sacrifices (Isaac, 1983). The warriors were taken alive to the Templo Mayor, a stepped pyramid placed in Tenochtitlan. At the top of the pyramid, the warriors were placed on the ritual altar (Milligan, 2023). There, five priests perpetrated the ritual. The victim was laid on the ritual stone, and four priests held him by the limbs, and the fifth priest opened the chest of the victim and took his heart off the body while he was still alive (M. Laser History, 2021).

The heart was considered the last symbol of life, and that's why it had to be taken while it was still working. Later, it was presented to the deity it was offered to and burned. Afterward, the body was tossed through the steps of the sideway of the pyramid, and everybody prepared for the next victim to be sacrificed.

This wasn't the only human sacrifice practiced by the Mexicas. Sometimes, people volunteered to offer their life or shed their blood to keep their gods pleased (M. Laser History, 2021). These sacrifices, volunteers, and Flower War victims' executions were always carried out as public spectacles.

Aztec's mystical practices didn't limit to sacrifices. They had everything recorded in several codices, many of which were burned after the Spanish conquest. Like many other American people, the Aztecs had a fascination for reflective surfaces (mirrors). They believed in the god Tezcatlipoca, also called "Smoking Mirror," who was capable of foreseeing the future and reading human beings' minds and souls. He was the god of night and sorcery (Maestri, 2019).

The Aztecs created mirrors from obsidian, a volcanic glass, and used them mostly for medical purposes but also as a shield to protect against evil spirits. If the spirit reflected on the obsidian, it was impossible that it could harm the victim. These obsidian mirrors, representing the power of the Smoking Mirror, were used by the Aztecs in the practice of scrying. The use of hallucinogens was also widely spread to predict the future.

Central America

Olmecs

The Olmecs were originally located in the territories of present-day Mexico (North America) and developed between 1,200 B.C.E and 400 in the surrounding area of the Gulf of Mexico, present-day states of Veracruz and Tabasco. However, they extended their trading activities throughout the Central American Isthmus to present-day Nicaragua (Cartwright, 2018).

Like many other cultures, the Olmecs believed in *therianthropy*: the ability to change shape and turn into animals taking their skills (Bowles, 2019). Among the Olmecs, the preferred animal was the jaguar (the largest American feline).

The Olmecs have left many records of human sacrifices in carved rocks, particularly in the valley of Morelos, in the village of Chalcatzingo. Many of these carvings represent people in the position of the victim lying helpless in front of those with flamboyant dressing, usually holding a plant. It is believed that it represented a ritual to pray for fertile crops. There are other pictures where the participants aren't people but figures with creatures half animal and half human beings. This has been interpreted as the souls that accompanied people during the rituals or shapes people acquired while performing them (Lambert, 2012).

There's a long tradition of witchcraft in the region, and even in the present, self-assumed witches, warlocks, shamans, healers, and psychics gather every year in March in the city of

Catemaco, Veracruz. It retrieves the ancient Olmec ritual of purifying the temple once a year.

Mayans: Sacrifices, Folk Healers, and Witchcraft

These people lived in tribal groups in Central America, in the south of present-day Mexico, Guatemala, Belize, El Salvador, and Honduras. They worshiped many deities that took care of their lives, and took care of them after death in the Mayan underworld, the *Xibalba*. It was a land of darkness and terror that souls had to pass through after people died. There, the souls roamed, and the spirits of the dead coexisted side by side with the living.

Mayans' most important god was *Quetzalcoatl*, the "Plumed Serpent," that visited the Earth twice a year, moving down the stairs of the Temple of Kukulcan, a step pyramid at Chichen Itzá. He was considered the god of craft. According to Mayan mythology, Quetzalcoatl made a monster called *Tlaltcuhtli* (or Cipactli), who lost its physical body. They believed the god came back every year searching for the lost body. The Mayans practiced human sacrifices to offer blood and hearts to the god and the creature to appease him.

Although Chichen Itza was a sort of marketplace, the place hosted a deadly ball game. Two teams confronted each other in a court twice the size of an American football field. The players had to pass a ball through hoops stuck on the walls. The losing team members were killed by the winners as an offer to their gods. After killing them, they cut off the heads of the defeated (Smithsonian Channel, 2019). The images of the winners holding the heads of their victims are carved on the walls of the pyramids.

This ritual recreates the mythical combat between two deities as it is told in the sacred book of the Mayans, the Popol Vuh. This ritual taught the Mayans to keep the balance between different worlds: The land of the living and the Xibalba.

The ball game wasn't the only sacrifice carried out by the Mayans. In the valley of Teotihuacan, Mexico, the human remains of twelve people were found inside the Pyramid of the Moon, a ceremonial center (Kovalchek, n.d.). Their heads had been separated from their bodies, and their hands were still tied at their back. In times of famine or when the season of rains was over, they picked young people, mostly slaves and children, and pulled them into cenotes: caves that were considered the gates to the underworld (Lucero & Gibbs, 1970). Many human remains of young people found in caves show evidence of violent deaths carried out as sacrifices.

Other sacrifices were less lethal but equally brutal. One of them was bloodletting, where people wounded themselves and shed blood as an offering to their gods. It was also called "auto sacrifice," and it could imply lacerating soft parts of the body, such as the tongue, the penis, or the ears (Kovalchek, n.d.).

Mayans also believed in and feared witches. The *wayob* were spiritual companions that usually belonged to animals and gave the witch supernatural powers. A witch could cause the death of an animal or even another person to obtain their soul and gain *wayob*. In Mayan societies, witches were accused of misfortune and tragedies. Many times, they became the victims of the sacrifices (Lucero & Gibbs, 1970).

Witches and sorcerers performed their practices in the caves. There, the *h'iloletik*, the healing shamans, used their knowledge to cure but also to take souls through witchcraft.

Those souls were sold to the Earth Lord, a malevolent deity who used the person as a servant. Those accused of witchcraft were used in funerary rites by the Mayan. When somebody died, witches were killed and dismembered. Some of the witches' remains were buried with the dead body, under the floor of the house, or left on the ground of the caves as "hasty disposal" (Lucero & Gibbs, 1970).

Mayans had the ability to predict the future. They were skilled mathematicians and astronomers and developed a complex calendar where they registered events that took place millions of years ago and others that are supposed to happen within 3,000 years. They also used their calendar to predict the future, similar to the astrological zodiac. According to their beliefs, the day of birth of a child could be under the protection of a good god or the influence of an evil one. That sealed the child's fate (Comunale, 2022).

This Mayan Calendar consisted of three circled calendars, one inside the other: the *tzolk'in*, the *haab*, and *La Ronda del Calendario*. They represent the energies that flow through the universe and everything that exists and affect living creatures, including human beings. The shamans had the power of divination and communicated with the underworld. They used La Ronda del Calendario to make prophecies and forecast the future.

The Mayan shamans predicted important events in global history, such as the end of an era and the beginning of a new one when Jesus Christ was born, the end of the Mongol Empire, and the Renaissance. They were even able to predict worldwide catastrophes like World War I and II ("Go With the Wind," 2021). Carved on the stones, the Mayans left seven prophecies that explain how the universe works and what will happen to humankind. The 4th prophecy is about climate change that is afflicting the planet currently.

The shamans also performed different types of rituals. One of them, which is still performed in the groups that continue to live in Central America and Mexico, is the *Temazcal* ceremony. In the past, it could only be led by women since the god Quetzalcoatl—god of death and rebirth—gave them the required power.

The ritual starts by asking permission and blessing of all the directions: North, South, East, and West. Then, the shaman bathes the individuals using steam. They boil the resin of a local plant called *copal* which has properties to purify the soul and body. Finally, they make an offer of flowers, fruits, and seeds to honor the earth. During the ritual, all the participants form a circle and place the offer in the center (The Jungle Journal, n.d.).

The Temazcal ceremony was performed in caves that were hermetically closed, lightened by the flames of a bonfire where volcanic rocks burned. Darkness and the atmosphere represented the return to the uterus. Besides the shamans, other people took part in the ceremony, beating drums and singing (The Jungle Journal, n.d.). The sounds, the smells, and the feelings of being enclosed and surrounded by shadows could only be tolerated as a community. That's why this ritual was a collective experience.

South America

Andean Highlands People

The Inca people lived in the Andean Highlands over 10,000 feet above sea level and built their cities on the slopes of the mountains in present-day Peru. By the 1500s, when the Spanish arrived in South America, the Incas had developed an empire, subjugating many other cultures along the Andes mountains in present-day Ecuador, Bolivia, Argentina, and Chile. Their culture was a continuation of another millennial civilization that lived in the region, Chavin, but very little is known about them.

Like most Native American cultures, Incas were pantheists. They worshiped nature: the Earth, the Sun, and the Moon. They believed the spirits of long-dead ancestors were embodied in the mountain peaks and rivers. Incas believed the creator of the world—*Viracocha*—was linked to the Earth, which provided them with everything they needed to survive; they had several rites and sacrifices to please him.

Inti, the sun, was the most important deity and the Incas carried out an 8-day ceremony to worship it in June, during the winter solstice (in the southern hemisphere). They held festivals that are still recreated in certain regions of the Andes, with different components added after blending with the Catholic conquerors.

Human sacrifices were common in Incas' festivities dedicated to Inti and the other deities. During Inti's ceremony, sacrifices and libations with water were practiced by the male priests and the group of young virgin women—sacrifices to honor *Viracocha* who preferred children. The executions were perpetrated by strangulation, and, as the Aztecs did, they would also take the victims' hearts (Cartwright, 2016).

Nonetheless, not everything at those ceremonies involved sacrifices, which, in fact, were reserved for times of crisis or after victory in a war. Incas paid tribute to "mother earth" with offerings such as "statues made of precious metals, finely woven textiles, and ceramics of distinctive Inca style, along with coca leaves, incense, food items, and alcoholic beverages" (Reinhard, 2016). They shared and drank *chicha*, a local beer. Some of these rites were carried out on tombs considered sacred. There, they buried food and goods close to them and later poured water on the place. They were careful not to disturb the dead.

The Incas had a particular type of sacrifice that distinguished them from other American cultures. They would compel people, often young women and children, to isolate in the mountain. Mummies have been found 20,000 feet above sea level in caves in the Andes slopes. The bodies of the victims weren't preserved due to special treatment like Egyptians did, but due to the climate conditions. The extremely low temperatures and the absence of moisture kept the bodies almost unaltered, and it was probably what caused their death (Reinhard, 2016).

Incas shamans were very powerful. In Cuzco, the capital of the empire where the Temple of the Sun (Inti) is placed, there were 475 shamans. They had the power to cast a spell and harm others, but also the ability of divination. Shamans could foresee the future by interpreting signs in the fire. They could also see or read the *llama*'s intestines.

Shamans were the healers of the communities. They received their power from their ancestors and were often revealed in a dream. As can be noticed, many common patterns exist among the different cultures, even though they weren't in direct contact. Inca shamans practiced a ritual on what was called *mesada*, a sort of altar. Around the altar, the shaman spread flowers, skulls, and other special ritual objects to invoke benevolent spirits.

The first part of the healing ritual was called "allowance" and it implies building a bridge between the conscious world and the supernatural one. To help the ill person reach that state, the shaman offers them a hallucinogenic beverage made from a local cactus. This drink provokes visions.

Then, the shaman starts the following stage, called *zingada*, to purify the patient. He pours tobacco and hot water on them to repel negativity and attract positivity. This part of the ritual usually caused vomiting, which was a good symptom as the person was eliminating the evil that caused illness.

Finally, the ill person was taken to the sacred lagoons with frosting waters and bathed there while the shaman said the prayers to their gods and ancestors. In compensation, people left clothes and jewelry near the lagoon (Proença Santos, 2017).

Among the complex religious practices and mythology, the Incas believed in the *huacas*. They could be anything: objects, gods, statues, elements from nature such as mountains and rivers, or ceremonial buildings.

Incas believed that *huacas* could foresee the future of pilgrims; people took offerings in exchange for helping them to make difficult decisions (Curatola Petrocchi, n.d.; Pinasco Carella, 2018). Oracle *huacas* consisted of special places, commonly caves. There, there was a sanctuary with a physical device, mainly rocks, and a person capable of transmitting to the people the messages the oracles sent to them.

Amazonia Tribes in South America

The Amazonia region comprises the Amazon River watershed and the Amazonian rainforest. The 2,400,000 square miles that it covers include territories of nine countries of South America (Bolivia, Peru, Ecuador, Colombia, Venezuela, Guyane, Suriname, French Guayana, and Brazil). Hundreds of different cultures live in the area, and many of them have never been in contact with Western civilization. This section tells about some tribes that live in the north and west regions, mostly in Brazil, Peru, Colombia, and Guyane.

Shamanism is a characteristic mystical practice of many of these tribes. They were practiced when the first Europeans reached the area and are still practiced in the present with very little difference since many of these tribes continue to live in the same environment, just like their ancestors. Unlike other cultures, shamanism in Amazonia isn't inherited within a family of shamans. Instead, shamanistic powers and abilities are acquired through conscious processes that can be led by a shaman in the family or anyone in the community.

As we have seen, most American people practiced some type of shamanism, sometimes playing the role of a folk healer and some others as a wizard or a sorcerer. Shamanism is actually practiced all over the world, and it has a double nature: it can heal and can kill. Amazonia has a great tradition of both light and dark shamans, though both can be the same person.

Dark shamans can be equated to witches and sorcerers in other cultures. They deliberately act to cause harm and kill others (Wright, 2004). Shamans are so powerful that they are capable of killing people—their enemies or attending to someone's request—at long distances through special rituals. Killing is, in fact, one of the main tasks for shamans.

Killing rituals are frequently targeted at the enemy, and shamans use figurines or effigies that represent the targeted victim. The different tribes give those figurines and practice alternative names, but they all are practiced similarly. They create a little statue and perform aggressive practices (dismembering the figurines, nailing sharp objects, or burying them) to it as they cast chants and spells (Temple of the Way of Light, n.d.). It is interesting to know that these chants and spells can also be used by anyone who knows them, even if they aren't shamans.

It was called the shamanic vengeance. Whenever someone was murdered, the shamans performed the ritual to kill the perpetrator. The shaman took a personal belonging of the murdered one inside a circle drawn on the ground. Meanwhile, the shaman pronounced a spell and burned the object using poison. In the ashes, the shaman could see the killer. Once he knew, he took hallucinogenic substances and would sing to find the soul of the murderer. Anything little that appeared at that moment represented the soul of the murderer: an insect, a bird, or a little animal, and the shaman killed it immediately. The person responsible for the death of the victim also died (Wright, 2004).

The light shamans, the good healers, practice a healing ceremony called ayahuasca in the upper Peruvian Amazon, but it was—and still is—common in all the region. The *ayahuasca* is a collective ritual: everybody in the community takes part in it, even if the patient is one individual. The main purpose of the ritual is to communicate with spirits to claim their protection, receive their wisdom to heal, and attract positive energy (Virtanen, 2009). Through this ritual, the community fights against the evil spirit that is always the ultimate cause of illness. The ayahuasca ritual is used to eliminate illnesses of the body and the soul and is also used for divination.

The ritual has a series of steps and requires complex preparation. This knowledge passes from generation to generation. The shamans led these ceremonies and reached particular levels of consciousness that enabled them to envision the evil, seeing things others couldn't see. This was achieved by a complex combination of hallucinogenic substances, dances, drum beats, and spoken magic formulas (Virtanen, 2009).

The hallucinogenic substances were made from two specific local plants that have psychoactive effects: the ayahuasca vine (*Banisteriopsis caapi*) and the leaf of the *chacruna* plant (*Psychotria viridis*) (Temple of the Way of Light, n.d.). It is very difficult to distinguish those plants from the others in a rainforest with 80,000 plant species. Even so, shamans had the skills to identify them and prepare them to obtain the expected effect.

The combination of the two plants drove the shaman to a level of consciousness that enabled him to see beyond the ordinary. Once reaching that state, shamans could heal, predict the future, communicate with the spirits, explain mysteries, prevent enemy attacks, and advise to make important decisions (Temple of the Way of Light, n.d.). The ayahuasca allowed the shaman to adopt the perspective of the animals, even though these Amazonian tribes didn't believe in changing appearance (Virtanen, 2009).

The ayahuasca was a thoroughly organized ceremony. It was carried out at night, when the village was calm, and the children (who don't take part in the ritual) were asleep. All the participants were aware of the procedures and each one's role, as it was a frequent practice. They sat on the floor in a circle and a vessel with the potion made of the *ayahuasca* vine and the leaf of the *chacruna plantis* placed in the center.

The shaman drank and offered the vessel to all those who decided to engage in the ritual and then smoked while waiting for the potion to act. After a while, the first effects of the ayahuasca potion became visible and the shaman started singing and pronouncing the spells to invoke the spirits from the animals and the plants of the rainforest. The chants and the songs helped the others to reach the hallucinogenic state as well, and the shaman had the power to raise the euphoria or keep the other participants calm.

Besides shamanism, the Amazonian tribes practiced other types of witchcraft and sorcery. In some Amazonian tribes, witchcraft is called *manhene* (in Portuguese, it is rendered as *veneno*: poison). The Amazonian tribes believed that the son of the god creator left poison on the earth as an act of vengeance for his own killing. It didn't only refer to deadly substances but to every act and object used to harm. Death was the ultimate objective but poisoning by witchcraft practices could also cause bleeding, vomiting, fever, and even behavioral changes. The most extreme was making the victim act like animals.

Witches were also called poison-owners and, unlike the rest of the people, had an animal appearance that could only be seen by the shaman. It usually was a human figure with monkey or sloth fur. Shamans performed rituals to extract the poison, mainly by using the ayahuasca ceremony and the ingestion of curative plants (Wright, 2004).

Sorcery was called *Hiuiathi* in the local language. It was practiced mostly through spells that desired and caused harm to others. This was a practice that anyone with the correct knowledge could perform, not only sorcerers or shamans. The spells were usually the same formulas used for healing pronounced backward and naming things associated with evil, such as snakes, scorpions, or the spirit of the dead. The spells could also be thrown at the victim with smoke or even be thought of, and it would still have the same effect (Wright, 2004).

Chapter 3: The European Arrival—The Impact on the Native Communities

The Conquest

This chapter will cover the history of witchcraft in the Americas when the Europeans arrived and the colonization process began. In the 15th century, the Ottoman Empire caused the collapse of the Byzantine Empire in Eastern Europe and became the new ruler of the Mediterranean Sea. The traditional commercial routes that took goods from Western Europe to the East—India and China—and vice versa through the sea were suddenly interrupted. The monarchies were desperate to find new ways to establish commerce. Back then, the wealth of the kingdom was supported by the amounts of metals collected from international commerce.

The Portuguese monarchy was the first one to venture into the ocean, searching for a new route to reach India between 1487–1488. The Portuguese ships sailed along the African shore through the Atlantic Ocean along the African coast, turned East at what present day is Cape Town, and across the Indian Ocean to reach the coasts of India. The voyage from

Portugal to the coast of Africa was enabled by the winds, but it was almost impossible to make the way back through the same route. That motivated them to venture to sail through the Atlantic and find better sailing routes (Encyclopedia.com, n.d.).

Some years later, the Spanish crown funded the project of an Italian sailor, Christopher Columbus, who had the idea to sail West across the Atlantic and complete the turn around the globe until reaching Asian coasts. He departed from the port of Palos in August 1492. On 12 October 1492, the three ships commanded by Columbus reached uncharted lands midway to Asia, their original destination (Calle, n.d.). Of course, neither Columbus nor anyone of his crew knew they had arrived at an unknown continent.

The Spanish fleet led by Columbus landed on an island of what, at present day, is the Bahamas in the Caribbean. The native Lucayan people called it Guanahani, but Columbus named it San Salvador (National Geographic Society, 2022). When they went back to Europe, these lands were called the New World, as those lands had never been explored by Europeans before.

The first to arrive at North America's shores were also the Spanish. In 1513, a Spanish expedition arrived in Florida (Georgia Historical Society, n.d.). Later, in the 16th century, French immigrants fleeing from Europe due to religious persecution arrived in Florida, and in the 17th century, they arrived in New England, New York, Pennsylvania, Virginia, and South Carolina when the English had already settled there (Encyclopedia.com, n.d.). The French made their first explorations in the mouth of the Saint Lawrence River. Some years later, the Dutch also arrived in America and founded New Amsterdam, which later became New York. The European powers also sent expeditions to the Caribbean and conquered islands there (King, n.d.).

The British monarchy didn't show interest in the new lands at first. They had a different strategy to expand their empire that didn't include conquering and colonizing territories and populations. However, at the beginning of the 17th century, many commercial companies emerged in England, with an increasing interest in the new potential markets overseas. First, they arrived at present-day Virginia and the Chesapeake Bay, and soon after, at the Barbados islands in the Caribbean (Encyclopaedia Britannica, 2023a).

The Colonization

After Columbus' first journey, the Spanish crown sent more expeditions to explore the so-called New World. Soon, they discovered the many resources that could be taken from the recently discovered continent. The Spanish, the Portuguese, the French, and later also the Dutch and the English didn't only explore but started settling colonies.

The conquest was the first part of the process. Not every encounter between the Europeans and the American people was violent, but in the end, the foreigners turned to violence to subjugate the local populations. Some Native people received them peacefully and shared the lands and the resources, and even established relationships with them. However, the Europeans soon realized that the local populations had solid and strong political organizations and that it would be very challenging to deal with them. Therefore, on many occasions, the Europeans faced the local people by violent means.

The colonization process of America began in Mexico by the Spanish, who spread along Central America, several islands in the Caribbean, and reached South America through the Andes range. The Portuguese also sent excursions to the New World and occupied the east coast of present-day Brazil.

In North America, the first to arrive were the Spanish to the peninsula of Florida, where they settled early as a colony. The French conquered the East coast of present-day Canada and the estuary of the Saint Lawrence River, and the margins of the Mississippi. France also settled in some islands of the Caribbean and the northern region of South America.

The Dutch also sent expeditions to explore and settle in the new lands. They arrived in North America, in present-day South Canada, and the mouth of the Hudson River, where they founded New Amsterdam (later New York). Like the French, they also took control of some islands in the Caribbean and conquered lands in South America known today as Suriname.

The British arrived in America later than the rest of the European powers since their colonial policy worked completely differently. They'd rather establish commercial bonds with distant territories and leave small administrative offices instead of settling colonies. Their first approach was through privateers' attacks on the Spanish ships taking goods and metals from America to Europe.

Nonetheless, Great Britain, under Elizabeth I's reign, also sent an expedition to claim lands in the New World. Sir Walter Raleigh landed in North America in 1584, and the first British settlement was established in 1585 on Roanoke Island. However, the British found a lot of resistance from the local population, and it took them a few decades to finally settle permanent colonies. Eventually, they settled on the East Coast of the present-day United States, the Bahamas Islands, and some territories in Central America (Belize and Honduras), the Caribbean, and South America (Guyana).

Each encounter between the European colonizers and the local population was different. Each colonization process had singularities that can't be covered in depth in this book. Suffice it to say that while the Spanish and Portuguese expeditions were financed by the monarchy, and the colonization process was led by the monarchs, the colonization that the French, Dutch, and British carried out—with the exception of the first arrivals and claim of lands—was mostly funded by trading companies with interests in the goods available in the new lands. While the colonization process was managed by the Spanish and Portuguese states in Mexico, Central, and South America, in North America, most colonies were a result of individual initiative.

The interaction between the European settlers and their institutions and the Native population had different impacts. In general terms, the Europeans imposed their supremacy over the local people. Despite the numerical superiority of the local population, the settlers ended up taking most of their territories, displacing or eliminating people, and destroying their original institutions and culture. Nonetheless, these local cultures didn't completely disappear.

The European impact on the Native American population can be summarized into three types of outcomes:

Suppression: When the Europeans eliminated all the existent society by annihilating the people or by compelling them to adopt the foreign culture.

Blending: When European settlers' customs coexisted with Native American people's way of life within the same society with both social groups or as neighboring communities. This persisted throughout several centuries. Several Native People continued to live as usual until the consolidation of the states in the continent after the independence process. Some of them remain still in the present.

Syncretism: This happens when two or more cultures mix to create new ways of cultural expression. It is specially used to refer to religious practices. Elements from the local civilizations remained and mixed with the settlers' beliefs and practices, evolving into new practices and providing new meaning to the old ones.

In general terms, the Europeans were horrified about many of the mystical practices the Native People had. None of those was considered a religious belief or spiritual practice. Instead, those practices were misjudged as witchcraft with the negative charge the term had in Europe by the 16th and 17th centuries. Europeans brought the idea of a traditional religion shaped by their worldview. The Spanish and Portuguese professed Catholicism, and for the Spanish colonization, the Catholic Church provided economic resources to finance the campaigns. Therefore, the process wasn't only colonization but also evangelization. The conquerors weren't only dominating to control land and resources but also to convert the Native People to the "real faith."

In North America, there wasn't a public interest or an institutional effort to align the new colonies to a specific official faith. Instead, the former settlers were predominantly Puritans, Calvinists, and Quakers, followers of different branches of

Protestantism who were fleeing from religious persecution in their countries.

Nonetheless, not all settlers practiced the predominant European religions. Many of the settlers preserved and practiced ancient pagan beliefs and rites.

Settlers' Pagan Practices

Magical practices had deep roots in European societies before they arrived in America. When the English and Irish came to North America, not all of them were Christians, and even those who were had several practices that were a blending of religious practices in Europe. For centuries, European people practiced some type of folk magic and witchcraft which later mixed with Christian traditions. The settlers brought all that to America, and for a while, both systems coexisted, the same as in Europe.

Those magical practices fall under the umbrella term "paganism," which is wide enough to encompass several practices. Paganism is a spiritual mindset based on pre-Christian spiritual beliefs and practices inherited by ancient people such as the Celtic, among others, that lived in Western Europe. It is difficult to define paganism as it overlaps with other terms such as animism, pantheism, and polytheism. It's enough to understand that they believe in nature as the major divinity and profess a deep connection with it through different rituals (Goodrich, 2015).

Regarding this connection with nature, pagans' rituals were carried out in open places and involved a collective experience. The rites were associated with natural cycles and related to the seasons of the year: birth and death, planting and harvesting, fertility, and thanksgiving. They celebrated festivals where people sang, danced to the beats of drums, ate, and drank. They used statues that represented their deities, including horned figures of fertility gods (The Pluralism Project, n.d.). Some of those coincided with the summer and winter solstices as well as the spring and fall equinoxes.

Paganism is based on these collective rituals and daily individual practices. Pagans' ceremonies started by drawing a circle on the ground. This was a "casting circle" that provided a sacred place to carry out the rituals. Inside the circle, energy rose, and worshippers were safe and became stronger. There, they could connect with each other and receive energy from the earth (their main deity). A worshiper can circle themself with silver or golden jewels for protection.

Inside the circle was at least one altar if it was a small ceremony and five if it was a big one, each of them pointing the four directions: North, East, South, West, and Center. Each of them corresponded to one element: Earth, Air, Fire, Water, and Spirit. The five elements are represented by the pentacle (an interlaced star of five points) that was drawn on the ground inside the circle but was also carved on personal objects. In addition, they also used a ritual knife or athame, the wand, the chalice, and the cauldron.

Even though most rituals are meant to be performed in groups, they can also be practiced alone. Many pagans have personal altars inside their houses or in the yards. On the altars, pagans leave objects that connect them with their power, crystals, photographs, and other ritual tools.

The rituals on the altars might be to speak or invoke their gods and goddesses, meditation, or healing procedures. They can also perform rituals for divination purposes. They might ask about personal concerns or what would happen the following day. They could resort to runes and crystals, a pendulum, and other objects to obtain the predictions.

To achieve a different level of consciousness, pagans might also make a charm and have herbal potions. In collective gatherings, that was achieved through the sounds of the drums and the voices and the dances that could take people to a state of trance. They also believed in the power of words. Therefore, the spells and formulas pronounced in group encounters and when performing individual rituals had great importance. They had verses and spells cast in individual and collective rituals.

Through the rituals, with the movements and the sounds, the pagans believed they could move the energy of their bodies and obtain more energy from the earth. That made them feel more powerful and capable of performing magic (Pluralism Project, 2002).

Witchcraft From the American and the European Perspectives

The arrival of the settlers altered Native People's life; their conception of witchcraft was used to understand the calamities that took place after the conquest. Through witchcraft, they found a way to explain all the diseases that whipped the communities introduced in America by the settlers, the loss of their lands, and the massacres they suffered.

From the European perspective, all Native people's spiritual practices were considered witchcraft. The fear of witches was brought by the Europeans from Europe and triggered when they ran into people with such different spiritual practices. The English, for instance, believed that the

North American Native People made noises during the rituals that reminded them of wolves and devils. They believed the Native people's appearance was the embodiment of evil. The Powhatans' main deity, Okee, was believed to be the Devil itself.

In the late 17th century, a settler reported an episode he witnessed. He told the story of a Native in North America who had an illness called "tormented" and went for help from the local shaman called Powaw. The shaman claimed that the man was a victim of witchcraft. The Native people that had accompanied him started dancing around the fire where the shaman was and accused him of bewitching the victim. The Native people threatened the shaman by throwing him into the fire if he didn't heal the sick one. Fortunately for both men, the sick one felt healed when he received the heat of the fire. Scenes like that one were frequent, and the settlers thought those rituals were necessarily connected to evil spirits.

Nonetheless, life in the colonies also influenced the Europeans' beliefs, some of which were similar to local people's spiritual life. For instance, the settlers believed that god sent them omens to guide their life on earth. The settlers also read the omens in nature through the phases of the moon or the movement of the planets. They believed that the crops should be sown when the horns of the Moon are up (when the crescent moon forms the shape of a cup) during the first-quarter shape because they believed the horns made the growth climb.

Despite their faith in the one true god, they brought several superstitions, which were considered signs and cues to prevent misfortune. For instance, they would avoid black cats or breaking a mirror. If they did, they would spill salt over their shoulders and be especially careful on Friday the 13th.

Witchcraft and Other Practices in America in the Colonial Period

The interaction between the settlers (with traditional religious beliefs and others with paganistic practices) and the local communities developed many new practices that gathered elements from both systems of ideas. Sometimes, the settlers adopted or respected the locals' beliefs. Nonetheless, on other occasions, Native American people were forced to embrace a new faith, most of the time under pressure. While some people made an effort to worship a new god, many others continued with their traditional practices secretly. If they were discovered, they could be accused of heresy. From the European perspective, everything the local people did was considered witchcraft.

New Folk Healers: Shamans and Curanderos

Health and the spread of unknown illnesses were major problems for the settlers and the local people who interacted with them. The living conditions were precarious, especially in the early days. Therefore, the role of the healers became central. The settlers had the dilemma of rejecting these heretic practices or resorting to them.

When the native healers practiced magic on the light side, the outcome was a blending of the original practice with elements that belonged to Christianity. Nonetheless, these healers (shamans for some, *curanderos* for others) could be associated with the dark side of magic and accused of witchcraft, even by their own people.

Curanderos (male) and *curanderas* (female) were typical from Latin America, where the colonization process was carried out by Catholic Spanish. The word comes from the Spanish word *curar*, which means "heal." The practice of *curanderismo* is still sustained in the ancient belief that illness is a result of an imbalance between the body, the spirit, the cosmos, and after the influence of Christianity, God.

The traditional folk healers continued to use their knowledge of the curative power of the local herbs and how to mix them to create healing beverages, but instead of spells, they could use Christian prayers or call upon the Christian god and saints. The traditional altars and rituals that included elements coming from nature were replaced by crosses, holy water, and Christian altars (Montiel Tafur et al., 2009).

Traditional shamanism included the use of statutes or little figures that represented the body of the ill. After the blending with Christianity, those statues were replaced by images or pictures of Christian saints, Jesus Christ, and the Virgin Mary. The rituals preserved many of the ancient practices based mostly on the ingestion of cold or hot food to restore the imbalance. For instance, a cold drink or a bath in freezing water could harm someone in a highly emotional state, and to counteract, the person received a hot potion.

Plants and herbs are used to prepare teas and potions. The leaves, stems, and flowers were mixed and boiled or used to make ointments (Montiel Tafur et al., 2009). There were (and still are found in Latin communities) different types of specialist *curanderos* regarding the methodology they use to heal (Cocking, 2017):

- *peyoteros*, those who cure by means of the spiritual hallucinogenic *peyote*,

- *yerberos*, healers who mainly prescribe teas and herbs,
- *rezanderos* and *oracionistas*, curanderos that pray in front of special altars, with candles and other ritual objects from the Catholic symbology.

This isn't only a change in the ritual objects but also in the beliefs beyond the practice. While before Christianity, the power of healers came from their wisdom or was a supernatural feature, after the blending, it became a gift from God (Montiel Tafur et al., 2009). It is usually called the *don* (gift) or a spiritual calling that makes them different from the rest of the people.

The curanderos/as could diagnose illnesses that involved the spirit and the relationship with others. The healing didn't depend only on the herbs, potions, and ointments but on the mystical power of the curandero/a. According to Leal (2014) and Montiel Tafour and others (2009), the most common diagnoses were:

- *caída de la mollera*: A soft spot on a baby's head, which could be caused by a fall or sudden movements.
- *susto*: This meant that the person had lost their soul. It happened when the soul left the body due to trauma, not physical but emotional. Somehow, this made folk healers the psychologists of the community in addition to being the doctor.
- *empacho*: An intestinal disorder caused by the ingestion of excessive or poisoned food.
- *mal de ojo* or evil eye: Occurred when a person stared at an ill person.

- *pata de cabra*: A disease that makes the baby pull their head backward and has a green or dark spot at the waist on the back.

These illnesses could only be diagnosed and treated by the folk healer. Diagnosis and treatment required different procedures. For instance, to diagnose the *empacho*, the healer took a strip and measured their arm three times. Therefore, the strip used for the next stage measured at three times the length of the healer's arm. Next, the healer would place one end of the strip on the ill person's stomach and hold the other end with their left hand. Then, the healer crossed themselves and extended their arm from the elbow to the tip of the fingers on the strip three times. Wherever they rested their fingers on the strip, that's where the next movement of the arm started. If, with the last movement, the healer couldn't reach the stomach of the person with their fingertips, it meant the person was *empachada*.

The healing process consisted of repeating this ritual three times. Before measuring the string with the arm, the healer would say secret prayers. The whole process was repeated for three consecutive days and could be complemented with herbal tea (Leal, 2014). The number three is considered magical in witchcraft. The healing process was thought to be effective if the folk healer yawned or felt dizzy while performing it.

The healer had a special power but it could be transmitted to others, mainly members of their family. The secret was revealed at a special or sacred moment of the year, such as Christmas Eve or Easter. It is believed that on those days, the distance between spirits and human beings shortens.

Pata de cabra is an illness that is, in fact, caused by a parasite. It could be easily diagnosed by the trained eye of the folk healer. The child with *pata de cabra* had a spot on their back at the waist or coccyx, where the parasite was hosted. From there, the parasite climbed through the spine until reaching the child's head. If that happened, the child would have died.

The healing process lasted nine days and couldn't be interrupted. If it was, they had to wait fifteen days to start all over. The healer gave the parents of the ill baby a bottle with oil. The parents made the sign of a cross on the spot with the oil, where the parasite was located, and using that finger, drew a line with the oil up the spine to the head. Meanwhile, the healer would help in the process from their home, praying during the nine days. After the healing process was finished, the parents had to bury the empty bottle of oil in a distant place (Leal, 2014).

The traditional folk healers, shamans, and curanderos continued to exist during the colonial period and until the present. Not all of them introduced Christian symbols and instead remained using ancient magical formulas and herbs. Nonetheless, all of them emphasize the link between the illnesses of the body and evil and consider the mind and the spirit as a part of the healing process.

Folk Healers and Spiritismo

Some folk healers didn't have the unique power to heal but also to perform as mediums with the spirits of the dead or with the saints. This was a special type of intercession carried out by the healer. It was (and still is) called *espiritismo*.

While most traditional folk healers and *curanderos* carried out their practices in a physical sense, spiritualists (*espiritistas*) had a superior power to communicate with entities beyond the material world. Curanderismo already required an active role of the patient who had to believe and have faith in the healing power of the *curandero*, there was still concrete evidence of the illness (for instance, the spot of *pata de cabra*), and notable results. However, in the case of spiritism, it was more difficult to offer proof of the actual contact with the spirits. Eventually, it was all left to the patient's faith.

Some spiritualists invoked the saints from the Catholic church, but not any saint. They had the ability to "see" the illness and decide which saint should be invoked to heal. The procedure to identify the proper saint could involve some empirical objects. For instance, they would put pieces of cloth or wood into the water to see which one floated. The spiritualists could make a pilgrimage on behalf of the patient to certain sacred places related to the target saint as an offer to ask and thank for healing (Sharp, 2005).

Espiritistas acted when the illness wasn't of the body. Instead, health issues were caused by spirits that could even possess the ill person. With a Christian frame, illnesses could be the result of a sin. Therefore, it could only be healed by the *espiritista*, and it consisted in removing the pernicious spirits from the ill person's body, and strengthening the positive ones' influence (iResearchNet, n.d.).

Another singularity about *espiritistas* was they could also contact other types of spirits, not only the souls of dead people. Those other spirits could be non-human entities such as demons and other evil creatures.

Folk Saints—San La Muerte (Saint of Death)

Saints are a figure created by the Catholic Church. They represent human beings that, by the power of their strong faith and some extraordinary experience through their life or death, have excelled as Christians. The process of considering a dead person a saint is monopolized by the papacy, and it demands the confirmation of at least three miracles. It is a formal process.

In times when faith faltered, the Catholic church would provide new saints as a way to promote saint life among the worshippers and the ideal of a better life in heaven after suffering on earth. Saints were always pious people who had a life dedicated to God or that had died in defense of their faith, but they were also ordinary people selected by God to perform miracles on behalf of his mercy.

However, people's faith couldn't be completely controlled by institutions, and popular saints emerged constantly in Europe and also in America after the arrival of Christianity. Folk saints are "deceased people, some of the entirely constructed identity, who are widely regarded as miraculous and receive the devotion of a substantial cult, but who are not canonized or officially recognized by the Catholic Church" (Graziano, 2006).

Most popular saints have had tragic deaths or were believed to have some sort of supernatural power when they were alive. There are dozens of popular saints in America, especially in Latin America and the Caribbean, where the Catholic church had a greater influence (Natel, n.d.). Since there are so many, this section will focus on a particular profane saint that has the power to perform miracles or to cause great harm if the preacher demands so. It is called Saint of Death or *San La Muerte*: The Lord of Death.

Like all folk saints, the stories of how they became saints and the miracles attributed to them are transmitted orally, and the versions are distorted throughout time. *San La Muerte* is worshiped in Mexico but also in Argentina, and in every country, the story of his life, death, and powers vary from place to place.

It is represented as a skeleton with a black cloak that covers his head and body (some affirm that, in fact, it is a female image) and holds a scythe in one hand and the world in another. Its worship is usually associated with people involved in illegal activities, and it is controversial because it is a saint that can protect and heal but also be used for evil purposes.

The rituals carried out by his followers include offers that can be goods, or personal sacrifices, depending on the requested favor. The more extreme the favor, the greater the offer. For instance, people might have to get a tattoo of the saint or some sort of self-inflicted physical pain. If the worshiper wants to give thanks for a miracle, they are expected to set an altar with candies, cigarettes, and some liquor (Pasciuto, 2023).

Altars are taken from Christian and other paganistic practices. Saint of Death worshippers also use other objects and symbols taken from Christianity, like rosary beads and votive candles. For the latter, every color has a particular meaning and purpose: red for love requests, golden to attract prosperity, and purple and white for healing (Pasciuto, 2023).

The altars must have a statue of the saint and must be placed at the worshiper's house or in a public place. It is very common to see these altars by the roads or in wastelands. These saints are rejected not only by the Catholic church but by all the traditional institutions. Therefore, it is a test of faith to publicly express the worship of this profane saint.

Chapter 4: The African Influence— The Impact on Local Cultures

At the beginning of the 17th century, people from Africa were enslaved and taken to America to work in the crops, the mines, and servitude. Despite the deliberate processes to deprive them of their identity as human beings and their cultural roots, they managed to bring with them their beliefs and spiritual practices.

Let's now discuss how the African enslaved people contributed to the blending between different beliefs and mystical practices that had started between the settlers and the Native communities. This bending didn't occur in the same way throughout America. Enslaved people had different means of interaction with the European and the Native population, and the cultural merge took longer in some places.

Similarly to what happened with Native American cultures, most cultural and mystical practices carried out by enslaved Africans were severely repressed. The outcome was that some disappeared, some blended, and many others were a vehicle of resistance. In the present, some of those practices endure with slight changes.

Slavery in America

At first, the Spanish used Native American people as their main workforce through different means of labor exploitation, similar to slavery but under other names and regulations. They were used in the crops, mines, and for servitude. But due to the extreme mistreatment that Native people were subjected to and the reports sent back to Spain by some Catholic priests, the Spanish crown prohibited slavery on the local population; therefore, the slave trade for Africa began.

African enslaved people arrived in South America at the beginning of the 16th century. The first arrival of African enslaved people in North America didn't occur until the year 1619, when 20 people were brought against their will to Point Comfort in the British colony of Virginia. Half of the total enslaved people were taken to Brazil, and another 40% were carried to other places in South and Central America and the Caribbean, to the Spanish colonies.

The slave trade was more intense during the 18th century, though less than 10% of the total enslaved population brought to America were brought to North America, to the British colonies (Mintz, n.d.). The Spanish also brought them to present-day Florida, which was, by then, one of their colonies. From then on until 1867, over 10 million people were captured on the African coasts and taken to the Americas as slaves.

In the colonies, they were forced to work under inhuman conditions and exchanged goods in the trade market (Mintz, n.d.).

As a part of the Slavist system, people were kidnapped, isolated, and transported in merchant ships to be sold in the market. They had a price, and it was based on the physical capacity to endure and work. Although the master had the power to kill their slaves because they were property, it wasn't frequent because that was a non-profitable decision. However, death rates among slaves were high due to the terrible living conditions and the hard work they were subjected to do. Thousands of them even died on the ships on their way from Africa to America.

From the beginning, there was legislation enacted to prohibit the marriage between Black and white people, and many other racist measures. In Spanish colonial societies, social groups were organized as a caste system, and enslaved people were below the lowest scale.

In North America, though the British colonies received fewer enslaved people compared to Spanish and Portugal, the enslaved population had a greater rate of natural growth. By 1850, three out of four of the enslaved population was born in America. Slave trade from Africa was prohibited in 1808, but local slavery flourished then. By the time independence was declared, around 50% of the workforce were slaves and this spread to the southern states. In the 20th century, African American were still a majority in South Carolina (Shah et al., 2019).

In most American countries, slavery continued to be legal many years after the independence process. The first country in the Americas to permanently abolish slavery was Haiti in 1794 after the enslaved people's rebellion that led to independence.

In Central and South America, slavery was abolished in the middle of the 19th century. Cuba, Brazil, Puerto Rico, and the United States were the last American countries to ban slavery (Kottke, 2015). Nonetheless, the level of impact of the African enslaved population wasn't only determined by the legal status of the system. In some countries, many of the slaves were sent to the first line on the battlefield during the independence wars. In the United States, slavery was abolished only after the Civil War, and even then, new institutions with white supremacy ideology and legislation to repress Black people's rights continued to exist (Shah & Adolphe, 2019).

The Influence of African Enslaved People in the Local Communities

The slavery system was organized from the moment people were taken by violent means in Africa to the daily coercion exerted by the owner to force them to work and accept the terrible living conditions. Slavery is against nature, and therefore, people fight against it, even if that means death. To avoid people fighting for their freedom, slave owners and traders ensured to separate families and mixed people from different cultural groups to obstruct communication among them. If they couldn't adopt a collective identity, it was less probable that they would rebel.

In general terms, it was an effective system as it survived over 200 years. However, enslaved people rebelled against their masters in several ways. The most direct was a revolt, which was more common than what is usually thought. They attempted to fly and, over the years, organized to ensure freedom—some of them through the Underground Railway to Canada, and others by sea to the Bahamas islands, where they settled in a free Black People country along with the Seminole people.

Enslaved people would also deploy minor strategies to resist oppression, such as sabotaging work tools or stealing from their masters. However, they had another silent way to resist through their cultural practices. For instance, they refused to use the Christian names the masters gave to them, tracked other family members, managed to gather with people from their villages, and kept their traditions—music, folk, and tales—to preserve their identities (Townrow, 2016).

They were forced to be baptized and adopt the Christian faith. Though most of them didn't refuse, most of them internally preserved their original faith and continued with the spiritual practices they had in Africa or learned from the older generations.

Magic and Cunning Folk: The "Conjurors"

African people had a very similar perception of magic as the European and European descendants did. Both social groups' ideas about magic and their practices blended and it is hard to distinguish which of them were previous to the cultural merge and which was the new product.

For African people, magic was an equivalent to the West cunning folk and not a synonym for witchcraft in the negative sense. A witch was someone who practiced magic to heal the sick and the bewitched, foresee the future, and induce love. Many African people called these witches "conjurors," especially the Black communities that lived in North America ("Cunning Folk and Conjurors: Folk Magic in Colonial Virginia," 2016). Nonetheless, there was a specific difference between other folk healers and the enslaved conjuror. The latter played a political role in the rebellion against slavery.

However, like cunning folk, conjurors created magical charms and objects. These practices were called "conjures," a particular method to provide a magical power through words and objects (Glossner, n.d.).

The majority of the enslaved population came from West and South Africa, regions where the local population converted to Christianity to facilitate trading with the Europeans. This means that this blending between African magic and Christian elements began before reaching the new continent, and the influence was also mutual. For instance, salt was a frequent element used in African magical rituals. Christians incorporated its use in baptism ceremonies on both sides of the Atlantic.

The conjurors blended their practices with Christian elements as the shaman and folk healers did. The charms could invoke the intercession of Jesus Christ or some of the Catholic saints. These charms were written on paper and were used as protection. Magical objects were also made to protect the carrier. They included sacred or magical words three times to end the message, and the words had a Christian background: "*amen*" or "*fiat*" (faith) ("Cunning Folk and Conjurors: Folk Magic in Colonial Virginia," 2016).

The amulets were objects empowered by the conjurors to protect the carrier. For protection and other purposes, those who practiced "black" or "white" magic were also used to bury these objects. Some of the most common was carnelian beads (a semi-precious gemstone) and oysters, usually objects buried in lands that once belonged to slave owners. It is believed that they did this to protect the houses where they lived, and the meaning of the ritual was associated with the life and death cycle.

Other frequent ritual objects were glass bottles with different stuff inside, mostly used as a part of a healing process. It included all types of pins and nails, which were also common in some rituals carried out by Native American people. The ritual objects were limited to the few items enslaved people had access to or which could be made by them. It is difficult to know if it was a result of the blending of the two groups' practices or if there were similarities between both systems. The bottles would also have some urine of the sick or charmed person, and the sharp elements were added to hurt the masters as means of protection ("Cunning Folk and Conjurors: Folk Magic in Colonial Virginia," 2016).

A variant of bottles were bags where the enslaved people, especially those who worked in the plantations, carried out a series of magical elements provided to them by the conjurors. Those elements were limited since the slaves had access to very few things.

If the bottles or the bags were meant to harm others, it was placed in the corner of the targeted victim's room or left in the road where they would pass by. According to Glossner (n.d.), the magical stuff included animals, important possessions, roots, powder and even dust and dirt, and could be placed in a conjure bag along with materials such as herbs, roots, feathers, rabbit paws, chicken gizzards, reptiles skin, as well as the hair, fingernails, or footprint dust of the targeted person (p.14).

Conjurors could also add a luck ball to the bag, which was a ball made of "knotted yarn and silk thread, red clover blossoms, tin foil, and dust, which contained the souls of their possessors" (Glossner, n.d., p. 13). The slaves gave this bag or the ball to their owners to obtain better treatment. If the slaves wanted to hurt the owners instead, the conjurors would introduce a salamander into the bag or a bottle. The salamander would find the way out and bite the victim, causing a painful death.

Some conjurors in North America and islands in Central America, probably from similar African origins, invoked the god Obeah. This god allowed them to create the conjures either as charms or objects. Other worshippers of the god Obbeah were Akan spiritualists and Obayifo, who prepared magical potions that could be used for medicinal purposes or for malevolent actions (Rucker, 2001). These potions could be beverages or powders. They were mostly made of plants, herbs, human blood, graveyard dust, and other elements. These formulas were retrieved and used in other witchcraft practices such as voodoo, *santería*, and *candomblé* (Rucker, 2001).

Voodoo

This is one of the better-preserved original practices that were carried out by the African enslaved people in America. Nonetheless, it was created through a process of syncretism, where the African practices were blended with the elements of Catholicism that were imposed on the slave populations in the colonies.

Its practitioners were concentrated in Central America, particularly Haití and Jamaica, the coasts of Brazil, and later reached the United States on the southeast coast, as will be explained when talking about the Creole people. In these countries, voodoo is still practiced as a religion. Nonetheless, enslaved populations in different parts of the Americas practiced voodoo (Voudon).

Voodoo is defined as an "assortment of cultural elements: personal creeds and practices, including an elaborate system of folk medical practices; a system of ethics transmitted across generations (including) proverbs, stories, songs, and folklore... voudon is more than belief; it is a way of life" (Radford, 2013). It encompasses a broad system of deities and beliefs.

Voodoo practitioners worship Bondye, the god creator and the supreme deity. In addition, they believe in spirits called Ioa, the good spirits of the ancestor deities. Each of them has power over specific realms of existence: love, framing, human interaction, and so on. Like Christians, they believe in the soul, which can leave the body during dreams and if an evil spirit possesses it. However, voodoo believers think that a person can be possessed by a demonic spirit or by an Ioa. The last is desirable since Ioas are the spirits of the ancestors.

The rituals were carried out by a voodoo priest or priestess. They were characterized by their secrecy. They involve talismans, charms, and amulets called Ouanga, and when they are used for an evil purpose are called *wanga*. They used the roots of a magical tree brought from Africa, nails, holy water and candles, incense, crucifixes (all elements incorporated after the encounter with Christianity), and bones (Legends of America, n.d.).

Voodoo rituals were very varied. They included spiritual baths, group gatherings to read, sing and dance at the sound of drums, and pray. Through these rituals, people entered a state of trance (Legends of America, n.d.). Voodoo practitioners carried out these types of rituals for different purposes: healing, protection, communication with the spirits and the dead beloved, and also to hurt others.

Voodoo practitioners use gris-gris, which enables communication between spirits and human beings. These gris-gris are simply defined as objects used for magic. Common voodoo gris-gris are dolls called *nkisi*. They are considered the embodiment of a targeted person, and the practitioner who has the doll also has total control over the person it represents.

The doll is usually small and made with soft materials, easy to manipulate. It is used to nail pins on it. Despite a common belief, it isn't only used to harm the person represented by the doll. Voodoo practitioners believe that these dolls have the power to act to their benefit, not necessarily by hurting or killing the other person. It is used to attend to personal needs and keep social order.

The zombies were other mystical creatures. Voodoo zombies are different from the fictional characters displayed by the Western worldview. For voodoo believers, these creatures are astral zombies, spirits that can be invoked by priests and priestesses. Zombies appeared like human beings and could perform as if they were alive, but their eyes proved that they were, in fact, dead.

They even developed rituals to create zombies. It is one of the most violent rituals and is called "*makanda*." It was used when a person was condemned to receive punishment but shouldn't be killed. It is requested when a person has been offended and searches for revenge. The offended person reached the bokor, a sort of popular trial, and exposed the case. If the accused was found guilty, he could be condemned to the zombification process (Vald, 2021).

The first stage of the process was to administer poison to the condemned. This poison was a combination of toxic substances. The ingredients were "dried frogs, various substances, dried plants, human bones minced into powder, poison ivy, and the toxin of the puffer fish" (Vald, 2021, para. 17). The mixture of poisons causes convulsions in the person, and stomach cramps.

Then, the toxin of the puffer fish made the person appear dead. Nonetheless, they were still alive, with their vital functions slowed down by the effects of the toxin. The poisoned person was then buried alive and would later come out of the grave. Even though the person could walk and move, the effects of the poison were permanent and caused severe damage to the brain (Vald, 2021).

Voodoo didn't divide between good and evil or black and white magic. Instead, they believed both sides are part of the same nature of beings and nature.

Hoodoo

This system of beliefs resulted from the syncretism between Christianity and African-American spiritual ideas. It was mainly practiced in Cuba, Haití, and the Southern states of the United States, but there were also practitioners in other countries of the Caribbean and Brazil. In some regions, enslaved populations were isolated from others, and that allowed them to develop singular practices of hoodoo, for instance, the Gullah people in the southeast of North America and in the Mississippi Delta. Everywhere, hoodoo was practiced in secrecy since it was censored by the slave owners.

Hoodoo is usually confused with voodoo or considered a branch of it. However, there are significant differences among both spiritual practices. Hoodoo practitioners believe in

Catholic saints and prophets and worship ancient African gods. For instance, they invoked Moses in their spells, and they read the Christian biblical book of Psalms. However, they didn't believe or include Jesus Christ in their rituals (Universal Life Church, 2019).

Besides the incorporation of these elements taken from Catholicism, enslaved people learned from the Native populations their knowledge about herbs. They called their practices magick, a different spelling of the word magic which is still used. Hoodoo practitioners also recur to healing rituals to get rid of physical pain or the malevolent effects of the conjures.

Instead of shamans, hoodoo practitioners had conjurors simply called "doctors" by the believers. They were in charge of the rituals to heal, free souls from spirit possessions, and manufacture the amulets for protection. However, the conjuror could also harm others in the community.

Hoodoo practitioners believed in spirit possessions and the possibility of forecasting the future. Their main tools to counter-rest the effects of bewitchment or pain were using herbal potions, water immersion, and charms. They also added other substances and elements: "roots, herbs, crystals, animal parts, and sometimes even body fluid, such as tears, saliva, urine, etc., belonging to the person for whom the session is being conducted" (Universal Life Church, 2019).

They also had a series of rituals that included music and dancing. One of those rituals was called the "Ring Shout" and it consisted of dancing in a circle in the counterclockwise direction (National Park Service, 2021).

There is a testimony of a hoodoo ritual being performed in St. Louis (US) in the late 19th century that helps illustrate the practices. According to the witness, hoodoo practitioners gathered secretly around a cauldron with parts of animals (frogs, snakes, and lizards). People were speaking different languages, which was attributed to a demonic possession. There was a hoodoo queen who conducted the ritual. People danced around the cauldron and as time passed by, the dancing became more and more frenetic, as if they were possessed (National Park Service, 2021).

Hoodoo queens and kings could fabricate goopher (also goofer) dust for protection or to "fix a person" (National Park Service, 2021). As it could be used to heal, it could serve to harm. The same means were also used to harm, preventing someone from walking or from seeing. The goopher dust was made of graveyard dust, dry snakes skin, ashes, dust of bones and sulfur, insects, herbs, and salt.

Enslaved people searched for the conjurers for help before fleeing. They believed the intercession of the conjurer would ensure success and protection. There was a conjurer in Alabama who prepared a magical powder for people who used the Underground Railroad to escape. The powder was made from graveyard dust that people rubbed on their bodies or clothes, which prevented dogs from following their scent. People said the doctor could "hoodoo the dogs."

Enslaved people also turned to the conjurer for protection from the brutality of the owner. The conjurer could tell if the enslaved person was going to be punished. If they were, the conjurer gave them protective roots that the enslaved had to chew and spit somewhere close to the owner. That appeased the anger of the owner and the punishment was less severe.

A branch of hoodoo had direct Bantu-Kongo origins. This branch of the hoodoo religion had a particular bag called "the mojo" or "toby" which served as an amulet. The conjurer prepared the mojo and put different issues inside herbs, roots, graveyard dirt, and other little objects. These objects were those enslaved people had access to. They were used as tools by the spirits that inhabited the mojo and provided protection to the carrier.

Hoodoo practitioners influenced by the Bantu-Kongo people also used a symbol in their rituals: the Kongo cosmogram or *dikenga*. It was drawn on the ground or any place where they needed protection. The symbol consisted of a cross mark or an X and it represented the energy that flows in the universe. One end of the cross represented the rising of the sun on the east and its setting on the west. The horizontal line was the limit between the world of living creatures and the spiritual world where the ancestors remain. The top of the vertical line represents where God is and his path through both worlds. Due to this belief in the cosmogram, hoodoo was usually practiced at crossroads, where it was easier to communicate with spirits and practice more effective rituals.

The Ring Shout was another Bantu-Kongo ritual among hoodoo practitioners. They drew a cosmogram on the ground and formed a ring around it. The practitioners danced counterclockwise in the direction of the movement of the sun rising on the east, passing through the sky, and setting on the west. The dancing created an energetic environment that enabled the dancers to communicate with the ancestors' spirits and also the Holy Spirit as another expression of syncretism. They danced along the ring until one of them entered a trance state and was pulled into the middle of the circle. There, the person was possessed by the Holy Spirit. The ritual was practiced to worship all the deities they believed in, including the Catholic god and saints, the ancestors, and nature. That allowed them to obtain magical results from the other rituals performed for protection or, eventually, harm others.

Hoodoo was—and still is as a minority practice—associated with conjure and root work. It remains a healing practice and also a spiritual expression of the African descendant population.

The Candomblé in Brazil and Rio de la Plata

The *candomblé* was a result of the evolution of the African people's magic and *conjurors* in America. It is an example of syncretism between all the social groups that coincided in that part of America. The candomblé retrieves elements from the Yoruba, Bantu, and Fon, Christian influence, and some components taken from Native American people. It has mostly spread through South America.

The candomblé has its origins in the forced conversion to Christianity by the Portuguese over the slaves in Brazil. That led enslaved people to accept the imposed religion publicly, but in private continued to worship their ancient gods and goddesses. As a result, their deities, called *orixas*, were represented by images similar to Catholic saints. The process of praying and the altars in their original spiritual practices didn't differ much from the Christian practice, so enslaved people could continue with their faith without being censored by the Europeans.

One of the most important deities for the candomplé was Yemanja (or Iemanjá), worshiped in Brazil, Uruguay, and countries of Central America. She is a Yoruba deity, goddess of the sea, saint of children, and protector of the fishermen. She was represented very similarly to Virgin Mary.

The candomblé practitioners carried out a ceremony to honor Iemanjá and asked for her protection on February 2nd. This is the day of the Catholic advocacies of the Virgin Mary, Stella Maris. She is the patron saint of sailors and fishermen. The enslaved people used the date from the Catholic calendar to honor their version of the virgin.

For the ritual, people dressed in white clothes went to the beach. There, they decorated the place to create a sacred environment. At sunset, they placed a sand altar with the statue or the image of the goddess and lighted candles. All of this was taken from the Catholic set of symbols (Zelenkoba, 2019).

The altar was decorated with fruits and food. People sat around the altar and waited until the moment the sun sat over the sea or Rio de la Plata (in Uruguay). Then, the festival began with the sounds of the drums, singing, and dancing around the altar. Some people jumped seven waves, asking for good luck for the new year (Rudy, 2019). The ceremony lasted all night, and at dawn, people put flowers on the surface of the water to be taken into the sea as an offer to Yemanjá, with a prayer for fertility and prosperity (Zelenkoba, 2019).

The *candomblé* pantheon encompassed many gods and goddesses, and each of them had a particular ritual. A person could request the special protection of one of those in accordance with personal goals or needs.

In addition to personal and collective ceremonies to worship the deities, candomblé also encompasses the practice of the *maes de santos* (mothers of saints), who have divination powers. These roles played by women weren't only used to predict the future but also performed as healers, counselors, and spiritual guides (Swift, 2017).

The candomblé also had priests and priestesses who had to pass through an initiation ritual that took weeks. To become one, a person had to go through a divination process to determine what type of role they should assume. Before being initiated, the applicants had to learn about the *orixas* (Yoruba people's deities: Obbatalá, Shangó, Yemayá, Oshún, Elegguá, and others) and the deified ancestors, and perform a series of sacrifices.

In addition to this ritual preserved for those elected to be priests and priestesses, candomblé practitioners carried out several rituals and ceremonies. In some places, they were performed on sacred ground called *terreiros*. Most of them include the sounds of drums, singing, and the intense perfume of flowers—all that created an intoxicating atmosphere.

Before the rituals began, practitioners had to wash their clothes and clean their bodies. They could prepare the ritual scenes in open places but there were also temples. When a ritual took place, the temple was specially decorated for the occasion. Some rituals could encompass sharing meals, divination, and animal sacrifices.

In some candomblé rituals, children play a significant role as they are capable of reaching the *orixas*, the deities. They would fall into a trance and communicate with the deities. The rest of the practitioners dance capoeira, a type of choreographed dance, as an individual way to reach the gods and goddesses.

Macumba and Sorcery

Before delving into these categories, it is important to point out the difference between sorcery and witchcraft. Both concepts refer to the use of magic indistinctively for good or evil purposes. However, while witchcraft is practiced in the community, sorcery is performed individually and usually secretly (Lewis & Russell, 2023).

The word macumba is an umbrella term that encompasses candomblé and other practices originally related to witchcraft with a negative charge. One of those practices was candomblé though it wasn't the only one. There were many others that also resulted from the influence of African enslaved people on local American communities, which don't have a particular name. Those practices are simply called macumba practices. Unlike candomblé, which is considered a religion, these other practices never reached any level of organization or systematization of their beliefs.

The term macumba has evolved through time and has been used to define rituals and festivals with drums and certain types of dancing. The macumba rituals are performed in sacred places, "the sacrifice of animals (such as cocks), spirit offerings (such as candles, cigars, and flowers), and ritual dances" (Encyclopaedia Britannica, 2017). Macumba are collective rites conducted by a medium who is capable of communicating with the spirits when they enter into a trance.

The word *"macumbeiro"* refers to those who practice the *macumba*, and lead the *macumba* rituals. They are usually considered sorcerers and feared by the rest of the people.

Quimbanda Rituals

The term *quimbanda* is closely related to the macumba, and it refers to another set of practices that involve magic but more specifically to black magic. In the particular case of *quimabanda*, the main purpose was to hurt or even kill a targeted person. The effect was obtained by certain rituals that connected the one who performed the magic with the deity that would enable the magic, and the one who requested the deity's intervention had to offer something in exchange.

Quimbanda rituals were usually performed in cemeteries and points where roads crossed. The ritual tools included dolls and figures that represented the body of the targeted victim. Then, the practitioners would nail sharp elements to the figure (similar to some voodoo practices). Another frequent practice was to write the name of the victim on a piece of paper and then put it into the mouth of a frog. As the frog died, so would the victim.

Unlike most of the other mystical practices, *quimbanda* was performed in complete secrecy. Nobody would admit to performing this type of black magic ritual.

Santeria in Mexico and Cuba

Santería was originally introduced to Cuba when the Yoruban people were brought as slaves from West Africa. Then, Santería was taken to Central America, Mexico, where it gained many followers, and the United States.

The word *santería* refers to "*santos*" (saints), and it represents a blended worship of ancient Yoruba deities (the *orixas*: Obbatalá, Shangó, Yemayá, Oshún, Elegguá, and others) and Catholic saints, produced during the merging process between the settlers and the enslaved people. *Santería* also receives the name of the "religion of the *orixas*" (Yorubas second deities), "Regla de Ocha," and the "Lukumi religion" (Carrodeguas, 2023). The Santería practitioners were called *santeros*, and had priests called *barbalaos*.

The process of syncretism was similar to the candomblé in South America. The Yoruba people accepted being baptized as Catholics but continued to practice their original religion. Therefore, they used the Catholic saints' names and statues to worship their ancient gods and goddesses.

Santería followers believed in the *orixas* (or *orishas*), deities inherited from the Yoruba people. According to Santería, the *orixas* provided the believers with protection and help in their daily life. The *barbalaos* were the priests in charge of the rituals to communicate with the *orixas* and acted like an oracle for the believers. The rituals of divination enabled people to communicate with the *orixas*.

The oracle (the priest or priestess carrying out the divination ritual) was called *Ifá* and was capable of interpreting sacred palm nuts. Through the voice of the oracle, the *orixas* could ask the petitioner to perform some type of sacrifice. During the ritual, the *Ifá* could reach a state of trance and act like a medium between the believer and the *orixa*.

The believers also had to present offers to honor and thank the *orixas*. Those offers consisted mainly of feasts displayed on altars in devotees' homes. People who were fully initiated in the practice of santería were capable of communicating with the *orixas* by themselves without the intercession of the oracle.

This personal and individual communication with the *orixas* could be performed by several means of divination tools such as the *obi* (coconut), *dilogún* (cowrie shells), and *epuele* (Babalawo's divining chain). The most important thing about them was how to read the *odu*, the signs sent by the orixas to answer the practitioners' questions ("About Santeria," n.d.).

Santería is considered a religion by their practitioners, and though they don't have institutions or written documents, they have a rich ancestral oral history. That includes *patakíes*, sacred stories that tell about their deities and rituals. Most of the religion remains secret but is accessible to anyone who wants to initiate into its practice.

The Creole People

The term Creole has many different meanings. It is used to refer to people born in America but descendants of European settlers. In Spanish, it is translated as criollo, and Créole in French. Within the colonial society, the Creole people had fewer rights than the Europeans who lived in the colonies. Therefore, this group had more direct and intense interaction with other ethnic minorities, enabling the blending of cultures.

Nonetheless, in some parts of the Americas, the Creole people represent a particular group with African roots who merged with the European population and Native American people. That is the case of Belize in Central America. In North America, there was—and there still is—a large community of Creoles who have African, French, Spanish, and Native American ancestors.

Most African people reached New Orleáns from Haiti after the revolution on the island. Hundreds of them had to flee after the revolt and brought with them their mystical practices, especially voodoo. However, the Creole culture spread through Central America and the Caribbean.

When the African freed slaves arrived from Haiti, New Orleans was occupied by the French, who attempted to prohibit voodoo practices. In 1803, after the purchase of Louisiana by the United States, Creole voodoo practitioners were free to express their spirituality. Then, the rituals became more visible.

The creole of New Orléans had a talisman called gris-gris. It was a bag, typical of voodoo practitioners, carried for protection or good luck. The bag was made of leather or a piece of cloth, and inside, it kept a paper with verses in the original African language. In addition, the practitioner put inside the gris-gris other magical and ritual tools. When gris-gris were owned by slaves, they were used as talismans to protect themselves from the owners.

The gris-gris, also called "gregory" or "gerregery," was also used as a birth control method. In the present, it is still used in some communities. For some people, a gris-gris is a symbol of black magic and is used to harm others.

The Creole community settled in New Orleáns and practiced a ritual with paraphernalia and the figure of the voodoo queen. It is believed that the voodoo practitioners carried out these rituals with orgies and people falling into a trance due to the sound of the drums. They were believed to practice human sacrifices, and people who became possessed moved and crept like snakes.

In fact, the snake is a symbol associated with voodoo and one of its rituals. One of the most important rituals was carried out in secrecy, at night, at the shores of Lake Pontchartrain. The Voodoo Queen, a group of practitioners, and a zombie were involved in the ritual. If there was no zombie at the place, they had a python, an animal they worshiped.

The group gathered around the fire and took the python inside a box to the Voodoo Queen. She took the snake out of the box, put it around her neck and on her shoulders, and let the snake lick her face. That way, the snake, the embodiment of a deity, transferred its power to the queen.

Then, the queen stood on the box of the python and started to shake and make singular movements. She touched the rest of the participants to share the power of the goddess with them.

The Creole people celebrate a festival called Mardi Gras. The voodoo practitioners wore their traditional clothes. The Voodoo Queen embroidered the beads herself, and each image had a particular meaning that represented elements of the ancestors' traditions. Women dressed in white would go through the streets, cleaning and healing by dancing and spelling conjures.

That festival continues in the present, and it is one of the many that combine elements from voodoo, Christian religions, and other Native American people's spiritual practices.

Chapter 5: Witch Craze in America—Witch Trials and Contemporary Persecutions

How Witch Hunts Started in Europe and America

In Western Europe, Catholicism spread during the Roman Empire and later, with the Romano-Germanic kingdoms at the beginning of the Middle Ages. Then, while some pagan practices merged with the Christian rituals, other ancient figures and rites practiced by native or Germanic people weren't easy to reconcile with the new religion. The Catholic church attempted to eradicate those practices and beliefs that fell outside their influence and were defined as heresy. That's when the figure of the witch emerged.

For centuries, witchcraft, folk magic, and other spiritual practices that belonged to the ancient Celtic and other populations that inhabited Europe coexisted with the predominant religion. During the Roman Empire, Catholicism spread over all of Europe but there was no censorship on these popular practices. On the contrary, both spiritual practices blended. However, by the 14th century, several social changes and the demographic catastrophe unleashed by the Black Death caused a deep moral crisis.

In response to this, the institutions and societies reacted, trying to find someone to blame for the calamities. One of the answers was witchcraft. Then, the term witchcraft was equated to heresy and malevolent magic. The idea of a witch resulted from some popular elements attributed to the folk witch and certain social prejudices.

Though there is historical evidence of persecution and execution of people accused of witchcraft, witch hunts as a social phenomenon started in the late 1400s and reached their maximum point of violence in the 17th century. The phenomenon started in Europe but soon it reached the colonies.

Accusations of Witchcraft

The witch was predominantly women, especially those who didn't fit into the social system. Widows or spinsters and women who couldn't procreate were considered useless to society. Witches were usually old and lived alone, many times isolated from the rest of the community. They were believed to carry magical elements, own black cats, and gather in secret ceremonies called the witches' Sabbath, where they encountered the devil, offered it their souls, and committed all types of atrocities. Nonetheless, a significant number of men were also prosecuted and executed for witchcraft.

There were several ways to identify a witch. They were believed to have a birth spot or a mark left by the devil on their body. Witches also had a familiar—a pet that was, in fact, the embodiment of a demon that assisted them in their magical performances. The most common was the black cat.

Other methods to identify them were more extreme. The accusers pricked or cut the supposed witch and if they didn't bleed, they were guilty. Sometimes, they used blunted elements, and therefore, the person didn't bleed (Nitschke, 2022).

Another cruel method was called "Swimming the witch" and it was mainly used in England and, later, the British colonies in America. The procedure consisted of tying up the accused and dropping them into a body of water. If the person floated, it meant they weren't a witch. If, on the contrary, they sank, it was considered proof of their culpability, and they were sentenced to death. Despite the final verdict, a lot of people drowned during the procedure (Dorn, 2022).

The Catholic Inquisition and Witch Trials in Europe

The witch hunts and witch trials started in Europe, but soon, the same procedures and ideas were transferred to the colonies in the Americas. In the late 14th century and the beginning of the 15th century, the Catholic Church created an institution to persecute and exterminate witchcraft. It was called The Inquisition. Bishops and priests that belonged to this institution were in charge of writing down the procedures to detect, prosecute, judge, and execute the accused of witchcraft.

The main manual was called the *Malleus Malleficarum* (in Latin, it means the "hammer of witches." It was written by two German priests and published in 1478 while the Protestant Reformation was taking place in Central Europe. This legislation and the procedure were implemented on both sides of the Atlantic.

The first systematic witch hunt began in Switzerland, in the community of Valais. Within eight years, 367 people were accused of being witches, sent to prison, and finally executed. The procedure to decide if the accused was guilty relied upon the testimony of the neighbors. If at least three people of the village admitted having seen the accused doing some magic, that was enough to condemn them. Since they were times of social unrest and confusion, people would provide testimonies based on what they believed they had seen or moved by the fear of being accused themselves.

The accused were subjected to painful torture sessions to make them confess they had a pact with the devil and had supernatural powers they had used to harm others. Under the coercion of torture, many people confessed things that weren't even true. In those testimonies extracted under torture, the accused spoke about encounters and feasts with the devil, rituals that included blood drinking and sacrificing animals and children, levitation, flying broomsticks, and night cavalcades, and even changing into animals. Those testimonies fueled people's imagination and provided new inputs for future accusations.

In the case of Valais, most of the accused were condemned to death. They were executed on the gallow or the stake: "Victims were tied to a ladder that was pushed into a pyre. As final mercy, the authorities tied bags of gunpowder around the witches' necks to hasten their deaths in the flames" (Nitschke, 2022, para. 3). According to the records, a big part of the trials didn't end in a death sentence. However, the number of people executed for witchcraft is still astonishing. The most admitted records say that between 30,000 and 60,000 people were executed for witchcraft in Europe between the early 15th century and ending of the 18th century (Kramer, n.d.).

One of the greatest witch-hunts was in Bamberg, Germany. A thousand people were taken to trial for witchcraft between 1626 and 1631. That process took women, men, old people, and children. From the total, 900 people were condemned to burn at the stake. If they confessed, they could ask for mercy and be beheaded to avoid a slow and terribly painful death (Nitschke, 2022). Fire was the main method to kill the witches because it had a purifying property.

The Autos de Fe Process

The Catholic Inquisition had a special procedure to prosecute the accused of heresy (Jews and Muslims) and witchcraft. It was called *autos de fe* and it was carried out in Europe and in the Spanish colonies in America. The last autos de fe was, in fact, carried out in Mexico in 1850.

The autos de fe was a public and spectacular ceremony with two main purposes: Condemn the witches and also show the power of the institutions and what happened to those who rejected it or didn't accept the Catholic faith. It was performed in front of the multitude and the local authorities.

The ceremony began with a long slow procession of the accused from the prisons to the place where they would be judged. There, the inquisitors read the accusations, and the sentence, followed by a sermon and the opportunity for the accused to recognize their sins and beg for mercy. If they did, it didn't mean freedom; instead, it only prevented the accused from burning at the stake and reduced the punishment to prison for life and losing all their properties (Encyclopaedia Britannica, 2014).

Witch Trials in Protestant Countries

Even though witch hunts were closely linked to the Inquisition, the institution created by the Catholic Church, witch trials were also carried out in Protestant countries, Scandinavia, and Russia under the Orthodox Catholic Church, although in a significantly lower number.

In England, witch hunts began in the 1400s but reached the highest point in the Puritan era, which coincides with the period of colonial settlement in America. In England, witch-hunter became a new profession. It was a person who dedicated himself to discovering and arresting witches.

Due to the imperialist relationship between England and the 13 colonies, the same rules were enacted in Europe and in America. At first, the settlers admitted the folk healers and Native people's traditional practices, but soon, the Puritan clergy started considering them witchcraft. Therefore, those practices were associated with the devil. Folk healers were accused of anything bad that happened to the community, and since they were small groups of people, it was very frequent that people accused their neighbors (Rossen, 2017).

The Witch Trials in America

Before Salem

The first witch trial in America was carried out in Connecticut in 1647. Five years earlier, witchcraft had been declared a crime, and the punishment was death. The first person to be prosecuted for witchcraft was Alse Young, who was condemned to die at the gallow. She was accused of an epidemic in a nearby village.

Before Salem, another wave of the witch craze started in Massachusetts that led to the prosecution of dozens of people. According to the record, one of ten was condemned to death by then. The trials were very similar to those in Europe, and the neighbors' testimony could be enough to send an accused witch to death.

The second death sentence was put on Mary Johnson in Wethersfield. She was condemned after confessing to having made a pact with the Devil. That was the first confession of that kind in the colonies (CT Judicial Branch Law Library Services, n.d.). The list of trials and prosecutions continued and expanded to other towns and villages.

Among the accusations recorded in Massachusetts trials, people accused others of making beer jump out of the barrels or bewitching the neighbors' animals. The interrogatories allowed the use of hot irons and boiling water to force the witch confess their crimes (Cavanaugh, 2016).

The Salem Trials

Salem was the village in Massachusetts that became the epicenter of a witch hunt in the 13 colonies. Between 1692 and 1693, about 200 people were taken to trial for witchcraft, and 20 of them were executed. The witch hunt was framed by social unrest caused by the war fought between England and France in the British colonies.

The first trial was triggered by the accusation of a nine-year-old girl named Elizabeth, and her cousin Abigail, eleven years old, started behaving in a weird way. In January 1692, the two young girls broke into screams, threw things, and contorted their bodies. Since there was no further explanation, the doctor blamed supernatural powers for the girls' condition. Shortly after, another girl experienced the same symptoms.

When the children were ill, Tituba was ordered to prepare a witch cake to discover who the witch was disturbing the girls. She mixed the girls' urine and rye meal and fed the dog. After the procedure, the girls said it was her. That was enough to accuse Tituba of being a witch. Then, the girls alleged she was helped by two other women Sarah Good, a beggar, and Sarah Osborne, an impoverished woman.

Good and Osborne claimed they were innocent, but Tituba delivered a confession of being a witch. She said the devil had come to her and asked her to serve him. She told the accusers the rituals she had performed with detail (Blumberg 2007):

She described elaborate images of black dogs, red cats, yellow birds, and a "tall man with white hair" who wanted her to sign his book. She admitted that she'd signed the book and claimed there were several other witches looking to destroy the Puritans (para. 8).

Tituba was taken on a trial a year later, in 1693. During the trial, when Tituba spoke, the victims (the three girls) stopped screaming, which was considered proof of her innocence. Then, Tituba said she could see Sarah Good tormenting the children. Then, Tituba claimed to have gone blind. The girls then said that they could see Sarah's spirit forcing her to confess (Women & the American Story, n.d.).

The following day, Tituba said that the Devil had made her sign with blood in a book where she could see the signatures of Sarah Good and Sarah Osborne. She told a story of how the three of them and many other witches gathered at her home and prepared a conspiracy against the Puritans of Salem.

Tituba was finally found innocent by the jury but had to spend a year in prison because she couldn't pay the bail. One day, someone did and she was released.

Many years later, after that confession, Tituba revealed that she had been beaten to admit being a witch (Women & the American Story, n.d.). Tituba's testimony was a trigger for massive paranoia in the village. From then on, testimonies from the neighbors increased against the women and pointed out other people.

Sarah Good insisted on her innocence but there were too many testimonies against her. The accusers were the same people that had helped her not long ago, but then they were telling the authorities that Sarah tormented the children by pinching and squeezing them and cursing them. Others swore to have seen her appearing out of nowhere and killing the livestock, naked in the night, or even flying (Rossen, 2017). Sarah was eventually sentenced to prison for life. Later, her little daughter of four years old was also accused and prosecuted for witchcraft.

Sarah Osborne was also taken on trial, and then she confessed that "in her sleep either saw or dreamed that she saw a thing like an Indian, all black, which did pinch her in the neck and pulled her by the back of the head to the door of the house" (Salem Witch Museum, n.d.). Ann Putnam, Sarah's neighbor's daughter, said in her testimony that she had witnessed how the specters of Sarah Good and Sarah Osborne had forced Tituba to go and cut her head off. In addition, Tituba had also given testimony against her. She was finally sent to prison and kept in shackles as the victims said she continued to torment them from jail.

The accusations in Salem continued and the authorities established a special court to carry out the trials of the local people and also those from the neighboring communities. Bridget Bishop, an impoverished woman with non-Puritan behaviors, was taken to trial and found guilty. Even though she defended herself on the trial, she was condemned to die on the gallows. That was the first execution of Salem.

The trials and executions continued until in May 1693, accusations were dismissed, and those who were kept in prison with charges and sentences for witchcraft were pardoned. However, by then, 19 people had been executed, one of the victims' husbands died during the torture session when they were trying to obtain a confession, and 5 of the accused died in jail while waiting for their trial (Blumberg, 2007).

Other Witch Trials in America

The Inquisition had the same power in America as in Europe. In Cartagena, Colombia, there was a massive witch hunt in the 17th century. Most accused were Afro-American enslaved people. There, autos de fe were used not only to read the sentence and the sermon but also to punish the accused, those who wouldn't confess their crimes, and also those who did. They received 200 slashes to pay for their faults since they admitted to being a witch or a sorcerer.

In the first half of the 17th century, dozens of people, predominantly women, were judged and taken in front of the crowd. Some of them were only tortured, others were executed, and many others died due to torture.

For instance, Ana de Ávila was a widow, the daughter of white and Native American parents. Although she was imprisoned and fiercely tortured, she eventually escaped and saved her life. Instead, Juan, a Black man from the Caribbean, was accused of sorcery, using herbs to kill people, and "teaching witchcraft to the Indians" (Dashu, 2000). He didn't even have a trial because he died during the torture. The punishers claimed that he had laughed while being slashed, a sign that he was a sorcerer.

Colombia wasn't the only country with relevant episodes of witch-hunts. In Venezuela and Brazil, witchcraft accusations were very common. The accused always belonged to the lower social groups, mainly enslaved people or Native Americans' descendants. Many of the accused were folk healers or had knowledge about the medicinal properties of the local herbs.

In North America, witch trials didn't only take place in Connecticut and Massachusetts. People were taken on trial in many other places, and the charges were always similar. They were accused of causing illnesses to others, and witnesses declared to have seen them interacting with the devil or performing magical acts. The "witch hysteria" reached the highest point in Hartford in 1662, when a girl died after accusing a neighbor of tormenting her with magical means (Woodward, 2003).

It is important to highlight that the witch hunt wasn't limited to the trials and the formal accusations. Even though the jury found a person not guilty, it didn't mean that the persecution stopped. The neighbors continued to exclude and mistreat those who were pointed out as witches (Woodward, 2003). It wasn't unusual for the same person to be taken on trial for witchcraft more than once. People would persist in their accusations.

Witch Hunting in the Contemporary Era

Even though the social phenomenon called the witch hunt that took place in Europe and the European colonies in America ended in the 18th century, the truth is that people continue to be accused and killed for witchcraft in the present.

In the present, there is a rebirth of spiritual practices that aren't restrained by traditional religions, and many people dare to express themselves in many different ways. Being a witch is, for millions of people in the world, something positive and empowering. Nonetheless, prejudices and fear of the unknown lead people to exclude and persecute those who are perceived as different, on many occasions accusing them of witchcraft and blaming them for individual tragedies or calamities that whip the community.

Witch trials were possible because the legal system of the era had declared witchcraft a crime. It wasn't only a moral prohibition but a legal restriction with an established procedure and punishment.

In the Americas, there was no specific legislation against witchcraft. Instead, the empires' laws were enacted. At the end of the 18th century and during the 19th century, American countries fought their independence wars and became free states. The new states didn't enact legislation against witchcraft. In North America, religious freedom was one of the main individual rights ensured by the political system.

Nonetheless, throughout the following centuries, episodes of witch hunts have taken place all over the world and also in America.

Lynchings

Since there is no legal frame to prosecute a person for witchcraft, a contemporary witch hunt is carried out by people in what is called mob justice. This implies that when a person is presumed to have committed a crime, people of the community will take justice into their hands if the legal system doesn't act. Lynching is one of the most common and violent methods mob justice employs to punish the accused.

Lynching isn't a way to administer justice since there is no formal accusation and no fair trial where the accused can defend themselves. This violent process might entail torture, hitting, mutilating, and even executing the accused. Witch lynching is still frequent.

In America, witch hunts still occur, especially in Mexico, Haiti, Bolivia, and Guatemala. In June 2020, an old man was burned alive in San Luis, a town in Guatemala. He was accused by the neighbors of being involved in magical arts and a mob of around 200 people sought him. The man's name was Domingo Choc, and he was a folk healer. The mob set fire to him and the man ran through the streets like wildfire while people shouted, "He was burned for being a *brujo*" (García, 2020, para. 2).

According to recent reports, more people have been killed for witchcraft in the last 60 years than during the witch hunt between the 1400s and 1700s (UCA News, 2022).

The Satanic Panic

This was a particular social phenomenon in the United States that wasn't related to witchcraft but to satanic practices. Nonetheless, this recent phenomenon reproduced the same pattern as the witch craze in Europe 300 years ago. Regardless of the number of practitioners of satanism or any type of magic, a lot of people were persecuted.

The trigger of a new wave of collective paranoia was a book that encompassed testimonies of rituals involving Satanist practitioners. It was published at the beginning of the 1980s and it unleashed a wave of renewed social hysteria.

The book written by Michelle Smith and her psychiatrist Lawrence Pazder told her experiences as a child in the hands of a Satanist cult. After that book, people from all over the United States shared testimonies of similar situations where children were captured and abused by people involved in some sort of satanic practice (Shewan, 2015).

There was an accusation on a babysitting service where children were subject to physical and sexual abuse. It was suggested that the place belonged to a secret net of Satan worshippers. Soon, everybody was talking about a Satanist conspiracy to invade American society, and services associated with children were the targeted places.

There have always been rumors and stories about the devil's worshippers and secret satanic cults. The difference was that in the 1980s and the beginning of the 1990s, people went to jail for that type of accusation. The charges included attracting and corrupting young people and forcing them to commit horrible crimes. The popular opinion linked satanic cults with heavy metal music and assured that the lyrics had a Satanist secret message. Dungeon and Dragons was considered a demoniac game and a way for young people to get close to those cults (CBC News, 2020).

Regardless of these arguments to support the accusations, the police and justice institutions interrogated children as testimonies for the legal cases opened to the dozens of people who fell under the accusations. Children, some of them as young as two years old, talked about blood rituals, animal sacrifices, and even cannibalism. Nonetheless, prosecutors and the police couldn't find evidence. Even so, people were kept in prison for years despite being innocent, or at least without being proven guilty.

The media played a significant role in the spread of social hysteria. The news reproduced the testimonies and the details of the rituals that were carried out. In the late Middle Ages and early modernity, it was possible that popular opinion influenced individuals to testify against others even without means of communication. With the larger scope of modern media, this phenomenon escalated quickly and all over the country.

In 1992, most of the cases were dismissed due to lack of evidence. By then, lots of people's lives were affected. In addition, the social hysteria began to decrease until finally disappearing.

Even though there are Satanist groups that consider themselves members of the New Age movement, none of them are involved in the rituals described in the accusations. This will be further explained in the following chapter.

Chapter 6: Wicca and Neo-Paganism in America—The Last Centuries and A New Era for Spirituality

Some social scientists have said that we live in an era of disenchantment in the world. So many terrible things happened during the 20th century that people no longer believe in a luminous future and are less likely to adopt any spiritual practices. Everything is about living in the present and experiencing happiness, mainly through material things. The evolution of technology doesn't give hope for a better tomorrow; instead, it tends to replace human emotions.

This pessimistic perspective clashes with the growth of a new spiritual movement that continuously gains followers. This movement can't be restrained to the traditional definitions of religion as a system of beliefs and practices with a unique institutional organization, a hierarchy, and a community of worshippers. In the present, more and more people are inclined to experience their spiritual life in a free way, based on collective practices or personal and internal rituals.

Witchcraft has always been part of our societies. While in some moments of history, it played a significant role for some social groups, in others, it was considered a crime. The 21st century witnesses a rebirth of witchcraft as one more expression of humanity. Despite the persistence of witch-hunts in too many places, people are progressively finding witchcraft as a way to experience spirituality.

This section describes new spiritual practices that have arrived in America at different moments and explores the contribution of all the cultural and social groups that blended throughout history. The umbrella term is the New Age movement, but there are two strong internal currents that have a well-defined identity: Wicca and Neo-paganism. The New Age movement represents a new blending between different cultural legacies and a combination of old practices and beliefs.

Neo-Paganism Practices and Beliefs in Contemporary America

Paganism is an umbrella term that encompasses different pre-Christian spiritual practices, including Wicca and other polytheistic and pantheistic traditions. Its origins can be traced back to Western Europe, before and during the Roman Empire, when local people's religion coexisted first with the Roman official religion and later with Catholicism. Even though those practices were censored and the practitioners were persecuted, these practices didn't disappear, and they have evolved and reached the 21st century.

The term "pagan" was used in the 14th century, and it came from the Latin word *pāgānus*, which means rural inhabitant or peasant. It referred to people not considered soldiers of Christ, someone who lived in the rural district and worshiped false gods and goddesses.

Paganism experienced a rebirth after the end of the witch craze in the late 18th century. By then, rationalism and science dissipated the attention to witches and displaced traditional religion from the center of social life. Nonetheless, people continued their spiritual practice and developed what is known as Neo-paganism. Nonetheless, Neo-paganism as a new religion has gained importance in the last decades, especially in the United States, the United Kingdom, and the Scandinavian peninsula countries.

This rebirth of paganism implies retrieving ancient practices and beliefs though adapted to the new environments. Neo-paganism is focused on a deep connection between human beings with the natural environment and continues to worship life cycles in nature. There isn't a unified pantheon of deities. Instead, each group or individual might choose their gods and goddesses. The common base is given for a set of values that encompass love and respect for nature, for others, treating people equally, and community life.

Wicca and witchcraft are associated with paganism since Wiccans follow a religion based on nature-oriented roots inherited from pre-Christian beliefs and practices. In this sense, Wicca is considered a branch of Neo-Paganism.

Main Beliefs and Rituals

Neo-paganism has a set of main beliefs shared by all those who consider themselves pagans, but there isn't a unified and pre-established liturgy of what must be believed. However, this common basis is what defines neo-paganism.

Unlike the Western tradition, they don't have a dualistic approach. Instead of opposing sides in nature, they believe good and evil coexist and celebrate both the sacred and profane. They don't consider that material things are profane and that souls and spirits are sacred. Life is sacred and, therefore, has to be honored. Their main deities are goddesses that can be worshiped with male gods beside them or not. They are worshiped following the cycles of life in nature and rituals involve magical practices.

Contemporary pagan rituals aren't too different from those practiced in pre-Christian Europe or by the settlers in America in the colonial period. Modern pagans offer food and drink to their deities while gathering in open spaces. It is more common now that pagans celebrate their rituals outside since there are fewer reasons to hide. Paganism wasn't meant to be secret (White, 2023).

Daily rituals are combined with festivals that celebrate special moments of the year, always linked to the rhythm of nature. That is the solstices and the equinoxes (White, 2023). To organize the festivals, Neo-pagans have The Wheel of the Year. It is shared by Neo-pagans and Wicca.

The Wheel of the Year represents the eight sabbats or sacred dates celebrated with festivals. Those sabbats are the four solar festivals (two solstices and two equinoxes) and the other four important seasonal changes. Ancient Celtic people also celebrated these moments of the cycle of nature.

One of the festivals is called Samhain, which means "summer's end," even though it is a few days after the autumn equinox takes place. It is celebrated on October 31st. This day is honored by Eastern religions with the yin and yang cycle, which also considers the beginning of the darkness. For Christians, it is Hallows' Day Eve since November 1st is the Day of the Dead, and November 2nd is All Saints Day. The latter is an example of how Paganism also influenced Christianity and its festivities.

Samhain, then, is a pagan festivity that welcomes the season of darkness as it isn't considered evil or sad. It is a moment of the cycle of life. Neo-pagans believe that on the night of October 31st, the boundary between spirits and the living ones is weaker (Mark, 2020). Therefore, the spirits of the dead can move into this world more easily. This isn't considered dangerous or frightening since they expect the spirits of their ancestors to go back to Earth and visit them.

However, the spiritual world is also inhabited by other types of spiritual creatures that can also enter this world and harm people. To protect themselves from those pernicious spirits, people use costumes and decorate their houses to keep them away. Bonfires are lit to symbolize the triumph of light over darkness. In the past, those bonfires were used to burn offal and bones of animals.

This is the background of the popular celebration of Halloween. It originated as a pagan festival to honor the dead. Now, it is celebrated by everybody, but it is also maintained as a sacred festival by Neo-paganism (Mark, 2020).

What Is Wicca?

It is difficult to find a single definition of Wicca. Regarding the core beliefs and practices, Wicca can be considered a branch of paganism. However, there are significant differences explained by those who practice it.

The word "Wicca" is usually used as a synonym for witchcraft, though that isn't completely correct. While witchcraft can be applied to name any magical practice, Wicca refers to a religion that started in England in the 1950s. Nonetheless, the word "witch" actually comes from "Wicca," an Old English term. So, it isn't totally unrelated, either.

Even though Wiccans might not feel gathered in a unified congregation of practitioners, it is actually considered a religion. His founder was the English servant Gerald Brosseau Gardner. The word was later adopted by Gerald Gardner, who is considered by many to be the founder of modern Wicca, to describe the religion he was developing. Gardner believed that the word "Wicca" was an appropriate name for his religion, as it reflected the ancient roots of his beliefs in witchcraft and magic.

After many years abroad in contact with different civilizations, Gardner went back to England and joined an occult community. Gardner claimed that there was a group of active witches near London, and they taught them everything he knew about magic. In 1954, he published a book, Witchcraft Today, and founded his own community of followers. From then on, Wiccan's community has continued to grow and reach all over the globe, including America.

Wiccans also recognize Robert Graves and Margaret Murray as the founders of the religion. They all had in common the intention to recreate the worship of Nature before Christianity. Strictly speaking, as it has been explained in this book, this worship didn't disappear but was blended or displaced by the majority religion.

In the 1960s and the 1970s, Wicca arrived in the United States and spread quickly, fueled by different social processes that were taking place. It was a period of confusion and social unrest. Witchcraft became a way to deal with the disillusion in Western societies and to confront the dominant norms.

In the United States, Wicca influenced the radical feminist group WITCH (Women's International Terrorist Conspiracy from Hell). The idea of the witch became a political symbol of resistance in what was then considered the second wave of feminism, just as it had with the African enslaved people that lived in the Americas. Zsuzsanna Budapest, one of the members of the movement, vindicated the women that had been killed for witchcraft in the past and used them as an embodiment of the patriarchal system.

During those years, Wicca also became an alternative for sexual minorities that were rejected from traditional religions. Wicca was a religion they could embrace and practice.

In the 1970s, books about Wicca were published, and as big parts of the population opened their minds to learn about it, others sheltered in prejudices. They accused Wiccans of Satanist rituals, influenced greatly by the Satanic Panic of the 1980s. Even though Wicca has usually been associated with Satanism and other occult practices, it is a completely different system.

Back then, Wiccans would follow their rituals in secrecy to avoid being discovered, like in times of the Inquisition. They gathered inside the houses and drew a circle on the floor, and had small altars that could be hidden anywhere. Many years later, they are now free to gather by hundreds in open spaces at the sight of anyone.

Later, a new perspective on witches reached the popular imagination through the media. Movies and television series projected an image of good witches and displayed Wicca's ideas and terminology. Wicca became more and more popular, and people started to practice it on their own.

In the first decades of the 21st century, about 1.5 million people considered themselves witches only in the United States. However, not all of them would say they are Wiccans. The Wiccan community has around 800,000 Wiccans (Berger, 2021).

In a nutshell, Wicca is a religion without the traditional structure. People who identify themselves as Wiccans join a community or practice it alone. Wicca enables a free individual interpretation of the ideas and beliefs, and although they encompass a community and have special rituals and symbols, they aren't restricted by organizational boundaries. Wicca can be considered a part of paganism, though not all pagans consider themselves Wiccans, and not all Wiccans name themselves pagans.

The popular imagination has created an image of the witch very different from the medieval folk witch. In the past, in the times of witch hunts, witches were mainly women and were below social expectations. In the present, males and females can be Wiccans, and for women, being a witch is a means of empowerment. What in the past put them in danger, in the present, makes them strong and powerful.

Wiccans' Beliefs and Practices

One important thing to remark about Wicca is that it remains a free spiritual practice. Even though all Wiccans have a common background of beliefs, each individual can interpret the ideas as they can or wish. Having said this, it can be pointed out that Wicca is a system of beliefs based on nature, and that's why it is considered a branch of paganism.

They worship nature in a wide sense that doesn't only include the natural environment but also human beings as part of it and the spiritual level of existence. The concept of nature for Wiccans is more complex than the Western definition. They recognize the influence of non-Abrahamic religions (Christianity, Islam, and Judaism), including pre-Christian religions of Europe (like Celtic paganism), North Africa, and Western Asia cultures (White, 2023).

It is a polytheistic religion. That means they worship several deities. The most important are Mother Earth, which, in fact, has many different names, and Father Sky. The latter shouldn't be compared to monotheist religions' god or heaven. Wicca doesn't have an idea of hell or heaven like these religions, as they don't believe in the opposing ideas of good and evil, God and the Devil. Instead, they believe in the existence of both sides in all the manifestations of nature.

Since it is an individual and free religion, a Wiccan can take gods or goddesses from other religions and use them for personal worship. Although it can be a solitary practice, most Wiccans join a coven, and each of them has particular features. However, this doesn't make Wicca a church.

There are many differences between Wicca and traditional religions. For instance, they have gods and goddesses, and all of them are equally important. Rituals can be carried out by anyone, though they have priests and priestesses, and unlike traditional religions, women are expected to adopt that role. In addition to this, Wiccans don't refer to themselves as believers but as practitioners, with an emphasis on the practice and the personal experience instead of the dogma or the ideological frame.

Since Wicca is a practical religion, Wiccans have a common set of practices and rituals. After all, faith and spiritual experiences are internal and singular. There isn't any regulation manual to attach to or an institution to administer rewards and punishments.

Even though Wiccans don't have a code of beliefs, all their practices are guided by a main principle. If someone doesn't follow it, then that person isn't a real Wiccan. That principle states, "Harm none and do as you will." As long as they observe it in their practice of Wicca, they can consider themselves members of the Wiccan community, even if they don't belong to a formal coven.

Wiccans perform magic which implies interacting with the so-called otherworld. They believe there is a universal energy surrounding living creatures and that energy can be funneled and used to achieve things. This energy can be attracted and manipulated to cause a desired effect on different entities, even oneself. Unlike other witchcraft beliefs, Wiccans assume that any person can learn to communicate with the other world and dominate energy.

One of the most important Wiccan practices is the rule of Threefold Return. It means that any magical act directed at someone will bring back three times the benefit or the harm to the caster. This is a self-imposed limit that encourages responsible and careful use of magic. Since Wiccans don't believe in good or malevolent magic, just magic, it can be used for any purpose. The limit is given by the counter effect that reverts on the practitioner.

Wicca has several rituals that can be performed alone or in groups. For Wiccans, rituals are always magical as they obtain the willpower needed to impact the environment of other creatures to achieve a desired change. It can be for healing, for obtaining things, or also to harm. That's why the rule of Threefold Return is key within Wicca.

Wiccans have eight festivals throughout the year. They are called sabbats which shouldn't be confused with the witches' Sabbath. The latter were witches gathering where they interacted in infamous ways with Satan and other demons. Wiccans' sabbats are just their periodic reunions to honor their main deities. Those festivals coincide with the important moments of the solar calendar: the solstices and the equinoxes. Those are the beginnings of the four seasons, a way to measure the cycle of nature. For Wiccans, this is a mirror of their individual life cycles. For instance, at the beginning of spring, they celebrate fertility in nature and in their lives.

The other four festivals are: "Imbolc, February 1/2; Beltane or May Eve on April 30/May 1; Lughnasadh, also known by its Anglo-Saxon name of Lammas or Loaf Mass, August 1/2, and Samhain, also known as All Hallow's Eve, October 31/November 1" (BBC, 2002, para. 8). In addition, each Wiccan has to honor their personal deity once a month when it is full Moon.

Sabbat festivals are carried out at night. They begin at sunset and last all night. They light up candles, bonfires, and lanterns. The Moon frames the celebration. If they are inside, they need a light that represents it.

These rituals are performed in sacred places outdoors, indoors, or in temples. They draw a circle in the ground, and even if they are in a temple, they'd still draw a new circle each time they celebrate. Then, the place inside the circle must be cleaned to enable the energy flow. The next step is to bless the place by naming the four elements and drawing an imaginary circle in the air with a ritual object. It can be a wooden wand or a black-handled knife (BBC, 2002).

Inside the circle, there is always an altar and other ritual tools such as incense, a chalice, and the pentacle. The knife is known as the athame. To perform the rituals, some Wiccans prefer to be naked, while others wear robes or their daily clothes.

The circle is cut from the environment with the knife and walking by the circumference of the circle. The knife represents fire. All the elements are invoked. Air is invoked with incense; water and earth are invoked together by pouring water with salt around the circle.

Then, the practitioners call the Guardians of the Watchtowers, the spirits of Ancient and Mighty Ones. There is one guardian for each direction (North, South, East, and West). The guardians are called to witness the ritual and protect the practitioners from harm.

Sabbats are a collective practice. All the practitioners gather in the circle and invoke the god or goddess they are honoring. To end the ritual, they share a chalice of wine and a cake. A similar ritual was described in previous chapters when describing the settlers' pagan practices, with slight differences in the procedure and the meaning. It is also possible to identify some elements taken from other religions.

Circles are included in every Wicca ritual. Wiccans draw circles everywhere, any time they need to perform magic. Those circles represent a special place "'between the world of humans and the realms of the Gods. Wiccans believe that the Circle occupies a unique space that is neither entirely 'mundane' nor 'otherworldly'" (Bado-Fralick, 2002, p. 50). The edge of the circle determines how the Wiccan behaves. The same person behaves differently outside and inside the circle and assumes a craft personality with a craft name.

The Guardians of the Watchtowers play a core role in the initiation rituals. They call together or summon the worshipers to witness the ritual and protect those involved in it from any harm. This ritual represents the transition of a practitioner to become a priest or priestess of Wicca. The Guardians are the facilitators of the process.

The Guardians invoke the circle through gestures and movements, prayers, and chants. Then, the ritual begins. The applicant is taken to the edge of the circle, but first, they are asked to provide two passwords: "perfect love" and "perfect trust." Once in the circle, a simulation of death is performed. One of the witches kills the applicant with a sword, and the applicant comes back to life shortly after. It represents leaving the old life behind and starting a new one as a Wicca priest or priestess. With their eyes covered, the applicant walks in the circle while the other witches say "neither bound nor free" to represent the new commitment (Bado-Fralick, 2002, p. 50).

The New Age Movement

This religious movement spread during the 1970s and 1980s and it proposes a new era of personal transformation and healing. In the last decades, the New Age Movement (NAM) has become stronger as they announce the global crises and social, political, and environmental turmoil are the prelude of a new era that will finish with this order and establish a different one (Robbins, n.d.).

Even though the main beliefs existed in antiquity, the movement as it is known in the present first originated in the late 19th century when Helena Petrovna Blavatsky claimed a new age was coming. She had founded the Theosophical Society, and she said that this new age would see the "theosophists (who embraced Buddhist and Brahmanic notions such as reincarnation) should assist the evolution of the human race and prepare to cooperate with one of the Ascended Masters of the Great White Brotherhood whose arrival was imminent" (Melton, 2023, para. 2). They believed that when the world entered a new Aquarian Age according to the zodiacal calendar, a new time of brotherhood and enlightenment would come (Melton, 2023; Dunn, n.d.).

Annie Besant continued Blavatsky's teachings and founded the Arcane School. She announced a new messiah coming and formed the "Triangles," a program to gather three people to meditate together as a means of preparation for the messiah's arrival. Members of the Arcane School spread their beliefs and practices and founded new branches (Melton, 2023).

In the late 1960s, the movement developed in America when Carlos Castaneda, considered the father of the contemporary New Age Movement, released a series of books about esoteric practices and shamans' teachings. Theosophist David Spangler also spread the message of a new era with waves of energy coming, determined by astrological changes revolving around the new Aquarian Age, like Blavatsky had announced almost a century before (Melton, 2023; Dunn, n.d.).

Main Beliefs and Practices

The NAM isn't considered a religion and it lacks a unified body of beliefs or rituals. It is a collection of similar beliefs that retrieve others taken from other religious traditions. However, the result is a completely different approach. New Age practitioners believe in one single deity, one god, and adopt pantheism as they believe that god is in everything, including the self of every individual.

Since divinity inhabits every person, it is a personal and individual responsibility to develop this divine nature. This encourages people to increase self-awareness and search for spiritual transformation (Dunn, n.d.). The New Age Movement claims that individual spiritual development will lead to a global new era with the end of humankind's suffering. This individual spiritual awakening is achieved through the *sadhana*, a path of self-growth and continuous transformation (Robbins, n.d.).

The NAM practices encompass two different types: occult and humanistic practices. The first allows the practitioner to contact entities from the spiritual world and even access it through special levels of consciousness. This can be reached by different means, including crystals, channeling, astrology, Tarot and other card reading, and many other healing practices.

The humanistic practices help the person to enter the *sadhana*, a path of healing and improvement, and keep them on it. These practices are focused on the development and care of the self. Through the self, the person reaches divinity. Self-awareness, self-sufficiency, and the development of the god element that lies in the self are achieved through yoga, meditation techniques, creating a spiritual environment, and being in direct contact with nature (Dunn, n.d.).

Many of these practices aren't only carried out by New Age Movement practitioners. Any person can have their fortune forecasted through Tarot cards or by practicing yoga and meditation. The difference lies in how people perceive their own practices and if they recognize themselves as a part of the New Age Movement. The core of the NAM is the individual spiritual path that will make humankind reach a new state of peace and prosperity.

Conclusion

Throughout history, people have searched for means to express spirituality. Many of them have joined traditional religions, but many others leaned toward other practices. Witchcraft, magic, and other systems of beliefs and rituals have enabled people to cope with reality, express their spiritual lives, and find comfort and healing for the illnesses of the body and soul.

For years, witchcraft and magic were considered primitive practices of less evolved societies. Now, it is better understood that these practices were carried out in every society in the world and history and continue to exist. Every society needs answers and solutions for chaos, uncertainty, and suffering. In the 21st century, it is already accepted that neither science nor traditional religions have all those answers.

This book has covered how American societies have searched for those answers. Before the Europeans' arrival, each community had its own system of ideas, beliefs, and rituals, probably influenced by the neighboring groups. Later, during the colonization process, those systems changed due to the interaction with the settlers. Folk healers and shamans were important people before and during the times of the colony.

Even though there was an imbalance of power between the settlers and the Native people, the result was a mutual influence. Even though the settlers attempted to impose their religion, many of them brought witchcraft and paganism practices from Europe. Despite the efforts to convert the Native people to Christianity, they managed to preserve their traditional practices. Sometimes, Native communities were forced to change their religious practices, but on most occasions, cultures blended and adopted elements from different social groups.

When enslaved people came from Africa, they brought with them their deities and rituals to enrich the local cultures. For many enslaved people, their practices were means of resistance. Nonetheless, it didn't prevent them from taking elements from the settlers' and Native Americans' cultures. Candomblé, hoodoo, voodoo, and santería are the outcome of this multicultural blending. Developed during colonial times, it has been preserved until the present, when the contribution of the African population to America's history is retrieved and valued. America's present identity is a result of the influence of three cultural backgrounds: Native American population, European settlers, and enslaved African people.

After centuries of religious intolerance that led to the witch craze, witch hunts, and trials that condemned people to death for practicing magic, the new generations are more open to understanding their spiritual lives, free from institutional boundaries and dogmas. Neo-paganism, the New Age Movement, and Wicca are proof that the present is deeply linked to the past, and people continue to search for ways to improve their lives and live peacefully and in harmony with their natural and social environment. Even though there are a few exceptions, witch hunts have almost disappeared in the present. People in America are free to adopt any religion or spiritual practices and don't need to hide from anyone.

Learning about witchcraft and all the different mystical practices developed throughout America's history is an invitation to embrace diversity and find a personal path for self-development and self-care. This is the key to thriving as members of the human race.

References

About Santeria. (n.d.). Aboutsanteria.com.
http://www.aboutsanteria.com/

Bailey, M. (2006). The meanings of magic. *Magic, Ritual, and Witchcraft.* 1(1).
https://muse.jhu.edu/pub/56/article/236416

BBC. (2002, October 2). *Religions - Paganism: Wicca.*
https://www.bbc.co.uk/religion/religions/paganism/subdivisi ons/wicca.shtml

Berger, H. (2019). Solitary Pagans. Contemporary Witches, Wiccans and Others Who Practice Alone. *Open Editions Journal.*
https://journals.openedition.org/assr/64019?lang=en

Besom, T. (2010). Inka sacrifice and the mummy of Salinas Grandes. *Latin American Antiquity*, 21(4), 399–422.
http://www.jstor.org/stable/25767002

Blécourt, W. & Davies, O. (2020) *Witchcraft continued.* Manchester University Press.
manchesteropenhive.com/view/9781526137975/97815261379 75.00013.xml

Blumberg, J. (2022, October 24). *A brief history of the Salem witch trials.* Smithsonian Magazine.

https://www.smithsonianmag.com/history/a-brief-history-of-the-salem-witch-trials-175162489/

Boas, F. (1914). Mythology and folk-tales of the North American Indians. *The Journal of American Folklore, 27(106)*, 374–410. https://doi.org/10.2307/534740

Bowles, D. (2019, October 9). *Mexican brujx, part 2: Shapeshifting witches*. Search Medium. https://davidbowles.medium.com/mexican-brujx-part-2-shapeshifting-witches-3998bd725c91

Breslaw, E. (2000). *Witches of the Atlantic World: An Historical Reader and Primary Sourcebook*. NYU Press. https://books.google.com.ar/books/about/Witches_of_the_Atlantic_World.html?id=1xloQgAACAAJ&redir_esc=y

Calle, S. (n.d.). *Historical Context of the Conquest of the Americas*. Columbia College. https://www.college.columbia.edu/core/content/american-indians/context

Carpenter, W. (n.d.). *Navajo Skinwalkers – Witches of the Southwest*. Legends of America. https://www.legendsofamerica.com/navajo-skinwalkers/

Carrodeguas, N. (2023, June 5). *Orishas y dioses de la santería cubana y la religión yoruba*. (Orishas and gods of Cuban santeria and the Yoruba religion). Norfipc. https://norfipc.com/cuba/orishas-dioses-santeria-cubana-religion-yoruba.php

Cartwright, M. (2013, August 1). *Quetzalcóatl*. World History Encyclopedia. https://www.worldhistory.org/Quetzalcoatl/

Clapp, N. & Patencio, F. (n.d.). *Desert shamans and sorcerers*. Desert USA. https://www.desertusa.com/desert-people/shaman.html

Cavanaugh, R. (2016, October 31). *The witch trials that America forgot*. Time. https://time.com/4543405/connecticut-witch-trials/

CBC News. (2020, February 20). *What was the Satanic Panic?* [Video]. YouTube. https://www.youtube.com/watch?v=plEImKEIRm8

Clifton, C. (2019). Review of "The Witch: A History of Fear, from Ancient Times to The Present," by Ronald Hutton. *The Pomegranate: The Internationla Journal of Pagan Studies.* https://www.academia.edu/41364349

Cocking, L. (2017, July 4). *Meet Mexico's Curandero Healers Keeping Indigenous Culture Alive*. Culture Trip. https://theculturetrip.com/north-america/mexico/articles/meet-mexicos-curandero-healers-enacting-surgical-miracles/

Comunale, J. (2022, April 8). *Mayan calendar predictions and accuracy*. Study.com. https://study.com/learn/lesson/mayan-calendar-predictions-accuracy.html

CT Judicial Branch Law Library Services. (n.d.). Our Libraries. https://www.jud.ct.gov/lawlib/history/witches.htm#:~:text=I n%20May%20of%201647%2C%20Alse,of%20the%20Old%20 State%20House.

Cunning folk and conjurors: Folk magic in colonial Virginia. (2016, October 31). Lives & Legacies.

https://livesandlegaciesblog.org/2016/10/31/cunning-folk-and-conjurors-folk-magic-in-colonial-virginia/

Curatola Petrocchi, M. (n.d.). *La función de los oráculos en el Imperio inca.* (The funciton of the oracle in the Inca Empire). Pontificia Universidad Católica de Perú. Academia.edu. https://www.academia.edu/5778832/La_funci%C3%B3n_de _los_or%C3%A1culos_en_el_Imperio_inca

Dashu, M. (2000). *Colonial hunts: South America.* https://www.academia.edu/9734901/Colonial_Witch_Hunts _in_South_America

Digital History. (n.d.). *Overview of the First Americans.* https://www.digitalhistory.uh.edu/era.cfm

Dorn, N. (2022, February 8). *Swimming a witch: Evidence in 17th-century English witchcraft trials.* Library of the Congress. https://blogs.loc.gov/law/2022/02/swimming-a-witch-evidence-in-17th-century-english-witchcraft-trials/

Encyclopaedia Britannica. (2023, May 19). *Cherokee.* https://www.britannica.com/topic/Cherokee-people

Encyclopaedia Britannica. (2023, July, 2). *American colonies.* https://www.britannica.com/topic/American-colonies

Espíritu Wellness Tulum. (2021, August 1). Temazcal ceremony. [Video]. YouTube. https://www.youtube.com/watch?v=IlPszoSiB3E

Exploring the Atlantic: Portuguese and Spanish voyages before Columbus. (n.d.a). Encyclopedia.com. https://www.encyclopedia.com/history/news-wires-white-papers-and-books/exploring-atlantic-portuguese-and-spanish-voyages-columbus

Farrell, D., Zunner, A. & Avetyan, M. (n.d.). *Witchcraft*. Pressbooks. https://oer.pressbooks.pub/beliefs/chapter/witchcraft/

French and Dutch Immigration. (n.d.b). Encyclopedia.com. https://www.encyclopedia.com/history/encyclopedias-almanacs-transcripts-and-maps/french-and-dutch-immigration

García, B. (2020, June 8). *A new witch-hunt in Guatemala*. Al Día. https://aldianews.com/en/culture/heritage-and-history/guatemala-witch-hunt

Gaspar, L. (2013). *Talismans and amulets*. Pesquisa Escolar Online, Joaquim Nabuco Foundation. http://basilio.fundaj.gov.br/pesquisaescolar_en/index.php?option=com_content&id=1310:talismans-amulets

Georgia Historical Society. (n.d.). *Early Spanish exploration in N. America*. https://georgiahistory.com/education-outreach/online-exhibits/featured-historical-figures/hernando-de-soto/early-spanish-exploration-in-north-america/

Glossner, J. (n.d.). *American conjure: African magic among American slaves*. https://www.academia.edu/32968443/American_Conjure_African_Magic_Among_American_Slaves

Go With the Wind. (2021, February 5). *The seven Mayan prophecies & the age of Aquarius*. [Video]. YouTube. https://www.youtube.com/watch?v=WnneTCu6PSM

Goodrich, S. (1859). *A history of all nations, from the earliest periods to the present time, or, universal history: In which the history of every nation, ancient and modern, is separately given.* Vol 2. https://books.google.com.ar/books?id=4w9FAAAAYAAJ&dq =who+did+the+russians+settled+a+kingdom+in+moscow&hl =es&source=gbs_navlinks_s

Graves, R. (n.d.). *Witchcraft & sorcery in Mexico.* El Ojo del Lago. https://chapala.com/elojo/index.php/135-articles-2013/october-2013/2241-witchcraft-a-sorcery-in-mexico

Graziano, F. (2006). *Cultures of devotion: Folk saints of Spanish America.* https://doi.org/10.1093/acprof:oso/9780195171303.002.000 1

Gutierrez, R. (2007). Women on top: The love magic of the Indian witches of New Mexico. *Journal of the History of Sexuality, 16(3):373-90,* https://www.researchgate.net/publication/24041971_Women _on_Top_The_Love_Magic_of_the_Indian_Witches_of_Ne w_Mexico

Hazzard-Donald, K. (2011). Hoodoo religion and American dance traditions: Rethinking the Ring Shout. *The Journal of Pan African Studies. 4(6).* http://www.jpanafrican.org/docs/vol4no6/4.6-11HoodooReligion.pdf

Historical context of the conquest of the Americas. (n.d.). Columbia College. https://www.college.columbia.edu/core/content/american-indians/context

Hong, C. (2020, March 17). *Rooting contemporary Latinx witchcraft narratives in the Latin American past.* Critical

Ethnic Studies.
http://www.criticalethnicstudiesjournal.org/blog/2020/3/17/
rooting-contemporary-latinx-witchcraft-narratives-in-the-
latin-american-past

Hutton, R. (2017, August 13). *Ronald Hutton on the witch.*
History Extra.
https://www.historyextra.com/period/medieval/ronald-
hutton-on-the-witch/

Inuit culture: History & traditions. (n.d.). StudyMaster.
https://www.studysmarter.us/explanations/history/us-
history/inuit-culture/

IResearchNet. (n.d.). *Espiritismo in Counseling.*
http://psychology.iresearchnet.com/counseling-
psychology/personality-traits/espiritismo-in-counseling/

Irwin, L. (1992). Cherokee Healing: Myth, dreams, and
medicine. *American Indian Quarterly, 16*(2), 237–257.
https://doi.org/10.2307/1185431

Isaac, B. L. (1983). The Aztec "Flowery War": A Geopolitical
Explanation. *Journal of Anthropological Research, 39*(4),
415–432. http://www.jstor.org/stable/3629865

Jaguar Bird. (2019, August 2). The Arawak people: First N.A.
indigenous people to encounter Columbus. [Video]. YouTube.
https://www.youtube.com/watch?v=0ZblVcXltcg

Kilpatrick, J.F. & Kilpatrick, A.G. (1970). Notebook of a
Cherokee Shaman. *Smithsonian Contributions to
Anthropology, 2(6).* file:///C:/Users/saifs/Downloads/SCtA-
0002.6-Hi_res%20(7).pdf

King, A. (n.d.). *French & Dutch colonization: 1607-1754 CE.* World History Encyclopedia. https://www.worldhistory.org/video/2377/french--dutch-colonization-1607-1754-ce/

Kottke, J. (2015, January 15). *A timeline of the abolition of slavery in the Americas.* Kottke.org. https://kottke.org/15/01/a-timeline-of-the-abolition-of-slavery-in-the-americas

Kovalchek, F. (n.d.). *Maya religion, gods, cosmos and religious rituals.* Maya Archaeologist. https://www.mayaarchaeologist.co.uk/public-resources/maya-world/maya-gods-religious-beliefs/#4

Kramer, H. (n.d.). *A journey into witchcraft beliefs.* English Heritage. https://www.english-heritage.org.uk/learn/histories/journey-into-witchcraft-beliefs/

Lambert, A. (2012). *Olmec ferox: Ritual human sacrifice.* https://www.rockartscandinavia.com/images/articles/a12lambert.pdf

Leal, M.S. (2014). La cura del empacho, el ojeo y el mal de Simeón en contextos urbanos de la ciudad de Santa Fe, Argentina. (Healing of empacho, ojeo, and Simeon's evil in urban contexts in Santa Fe city, Argentina). *Ëa Journal, 6*(2), pp. 95-120. http://www.ea-journal.com/images/Art06.02/Leal-Empacho-ojeo-y-mal-de-Simeon.pdf

Legends of America. (n.d.). *Voodoo Still Lives in America.* https://www.legendsofamerica.com/voodoo-america/#:~:text=Voodoo

Lewis, I.M. & Russell, J.B. (2023, June 21). *Witchcraft.* Encyclopedia Britannica.
https://www.britannica.com/topic/witchcraft

Lucero, L. & Gibbs, S. (1970). The creation and sacrifice of witches in classic Maya society. In: *New Perspectives on Human Sacrifice and Ritual Body Treatments in Ancient Maya Society* (pp. 45-73).
https://link.springer.com/chapter/10.1007/978-0-387-48871-4_3

M. Laser History. (2021, November 22). *Aztec human sacrifices.* [Video]. YouTube.
https://www.youtube.com/watch?v=or6W4sXpl3c

Maculotti, M. (2018, November 15). *Folklore, shamanism and "witchcraft" among the Inuit of the Arctic.* Axis Mundi.
https://axismundi.blog/en/2018/11/15/folklore-shamanism-and-witchcraft-among-the-Inuit-of-the-arctic/

Machi Francisca Linconao. (2018, May 10). Front Line Defenders.
https://www.frontlinedefenders.org/en/profile/machi-francisca-linconao

Maestri, N. (2019, July 3). *Tezcatlipoca: Aztec God of Night and Smoking Mirrors.* ThoughtCo.
https://www.thoughtco.com/tezcatlipoca-aztec-god-of-night-172964

Magliocco, S. (2009). *In search of the roots of Stregheria.* Academia.edu.
https://www.academia.edu/47503101/In_Search_of_the_Roots_of_Stregheria

Mark, J. (2012, July 7). *The Mayan pantheon: The many gods of the Maya.* World History Encyclopedia. https://www.worldhistory.org/article/415/the-mayan-pantheon-the-many-gods-of-the-maya/

Mark, J. (2020, December 31). *The ancient Celtic roots of the Neo-Pagan wheel of the year.* Brewminate. https://brewminate.com/the-ancient-celtic-roots-of-the-neo-pagan-wheel-of-the-year/

Merkur, D. (n.d.). *Contrary to nature: Inuit conceptions of witchcraft.* file:///C:/Users/saifs/Downloads/67169-Article%20Text-81055-1-10-20171119%20(3).pdf

Milligan, M. (2023, February 19). *The Aztec flower wars.* Heritage Daily. https://www.heritagedaily.com/2023/02/the-aztec-flower-wars/146236

Mintz, S. (n.d.). *Historical context: Facts about the slave trade and slavery.* Gilder Lehrman Institute of American History. https://www.gilderlehrman.org/history-resources/teacher-resources/historical-context-facts-about-slave-trade-and-slavery

Mooney, James. Sacred Formulas Of The Cherokees. Published in the Seventh Annual Report, Bureau of Ethnology, pp. 301-399. 1886. https://accessgenealogy.com/native/shamans-in-cherokee-culture.htm

Montiel Tafur, M., Crowe, T. & Torres, E. (2009, March 1). A review of curanderismo and healing practices among Mexicans and Mexican Americans. *Occupational Therapy International, 16*(1), pp. 82-88. https://www.semanticscholar.org/paper/A-review-of-

curanderismo-and-healing-practices-and-Tafur-
Crowe/8675b23c30c9ea7a00f1f05ec11c30c0a914c15f

Nail, K. (2018) *The structural violence of Maya sacrifice: A case study of ritualized human sacrifice at Midnight Terror Cave, Belize.* [Dissertation at University of New Mexico]. https://core.ac.uk/download/pdf/160274558.pdf

Natel, A. (2023, June 22). *Folk saints in the folk Catholicism of the Americas.* Scribd. https://es.scribd.com/document/498487872/Folk-Saints-in-the-folk-Catholicism-of-the-Americas#

National Geographic Education. (n.d.). *Aztec civilization.* https://education.nationalgeographic.org/resource/aztec-civilization/

National Geographic Society. (2022, May 19). *Oct 12, 1492 CE: Columbus makes landfall in the Caribbean.* https://education.nationalgeographic.org/resource/columbus -makes-landfall-caribbean/

National Park Service. (2021, November 23). *Hoodoo in St. Louis: An African American religious tradition (US).* https://www.nps.gov/articles/000/hoodoo-in-st-louis-an-african-american-religious-tradition.htm

Navajo People. (n.d.). Utah.com. https://www.utah.com/things-to-do/attractions/culture/navajo-people/

Navajo History Timeline. (n.d.). *Navajo People.* http://navajopeople.org/blog/navajo-history/

Nitschke, L. (2022, February 13). *European witch-hunting (A brief history)*. The Collector. https://www.thecollector.com/european-witch-hunting/

Palmer, T. (1974). *An examination of Navaho witchcraft and its influence on the thoughts and actions of the Navaho people*. Digital Commons. https://digitalcommons.usu.edu/cgi/viewcontent.cgi?article= 1968&context=gradreports

Pasciuto, G. (2023, May 8). *La Santa Muerte: Mexico's macabre religion at odds with the Church*. The Collector. https://www.thecollector.com/la-santa-muerte-religion/

Petersen, D. (2020, November 27). *Healing ways of the Indigenous Navajo people*. American College of Healthcare Sciences. https://achs.edu/blog/2020/11/27/native-american-navajo-medicine/

Pinasco Carella, A. (2018). *Oráculos, peregrinos y calendarios en el Santuario de Pachacamac*. (Oracles, pilgrims, and calendars in the Pachacamac sanctuary). https://doi.org/10.31381/pluriversidad.v1i1.1677

Proença Santos, A. (2017, February 17). *The witch doctors of northern Peru*. BBC. https://www.bbc.com/travel/article/20170214-the-witch-doctors-of-northern-peru

Radford, B. (2013, October 30). *Voodoo: Facts about misunderstood religion*. Live Science. https://www.livescience.com/40803-voodoo-facts.html

Reinhard, J. (2016). Frozen mummies of the Andes. *Expedition*, 58(2). Penn Museum.

https://www.penn.museum/sites/expedition/frozen-mummies-of-the-andes/

Rosen, M. (2017). A feminist perspective on the history of women as witches. *Dissenting Voices*, V. 6. https://soar.suny.edu/bitstream/handle/20.500.12648/2749/dissentingvoices/vol6/iss1/5/fulltext%20%281%29.pdf?sequence=1&isAllowed=y

Rucker, W. (2001). Conjure, magic, and power: The influence of Afro-Atlantic religious practices on slave resistance and rebellion. *Journal of Black Studies*, 32(1), pp. 84-103. https://www.academia.edu/223274/_Conjure_Magic_and_Power_The_Influence_of_Afro_Atlantic_Religious_Practices_on_Slave_Resistance_and_Rebellion_2001_

Rudy, L. (2019, August 5). *What Is Candomblé? Beliefs and history*. Learn Religions. https://www.learnreligions.com/candomble-4692500

Salem Witch Museum. (n.d.). *Sarah Osborne House*. https://salemwitchmuseum.com/locations/sarah-osborne-house/

Schoonmaker, J. (2015, March 15). *The Witches' Sabbath*. Manchester Historian. https://manchesterhistorian.com/2015/the-witches-sabbath/

Shah, K., Adolphe, J., & Kolchin, P. (2019, August 16). *400 years since slavery: a timeline of American history*. The Guardian. https://www.theguardian.com/news/2019/aug/15/400-years-since-slavery-timeline#:~:text=This%20is%20part%20of%20a,the%20era%20of%20American%20slavery.

Sharp, L. (2005). Popular Healing in a Rational Age: Spiritism as Folklore and Medicine. *Journal of the Western Society for French History.* https://quod.lib.umich.edu/w/wsfh/0642292.0033.019/--popular-healing-in-a-rational-age-spiritism-as-folklore?rgn=main;view=fulltext

Shewan, D. (2017, June 14). *Conviction of things not seen: The unique American myth of Satanic cults.* Pacific Standard. https://psmag.com/social-justice/make-a-cross-with-your-fingers-its-the-satanic-panic

Smithsonian Channel. (2019, February 22). *How this Mayan legend inspired a deadly ballgame.* [Video]. YouTube. https://www.youtube.com/watch?v=VYcWs7qJeCI

Swift, J. (2017, June 15). *Candomblé, Afro-Brazilian women, and African religiosity in Brazil.* Black Perspectives. https://www.aaihs.org/candomble-afro-brazilian-women-and-african-religiosity-in-brazil/

Tangherlini, T. (2000). "How Do You Know She's a Witch?": Witches, Cunning Folk, and Competition in Denmark. *Western Folklore. 59(¾),* 279-303. https://www.jstor.org/stable/1500237?origin=crossref

Temple of the Way of Light. (n.d.). *Shamanic healing - Ayahuasca & Amazonian shamanism.* https://templeofthewayoflight.org/shamanism-ayahuasca/ayahuasca-and-amazonian-shamanism/

The Jungle Journal. (n.d.). *The Ritual of Temazcal.* https://itsthejunglejournal.com/historias/temazcal-purificacion-y-vuelta-a-nacer/?lang=es

The Pluralism Project. (n.d.). Ancient roots, historical challenges. Harvard University. https://pluralism.org/ancient-roots-historical-challenges

Townrow, S. (2016, February 17). *Slave resistance.* Gilder Lehrman Institute of American History. https://www.gilderlehrman.org/news/slave-resistance

UCA News. (2022, August 11). *Witch hunts on the rise worldwide.* https://www.ucanews.com/news/witch-hunts-on-the-rise-worldwide/98356

Universal Life Church. (2019, October 28). *Voodoo vs. Hoodoo: What's the difference?* https://www.ulc.org/ulc-blog/voodoo-vs-hoodoo-whats-the-difference

Virtanen, P. (2009). *Shamanism and indigenous youthhood in the Brazilian Amazon.* Periódicos UFPA. https://periodicos.ufpa.br/index.php/amazonica/article/view/146/250

Waterman, H. (2017) *Herbs & verbs: How to do witchcraft for real.* daily.jstor.org. daily.jstor.org/herbs-verbs-how-to-do-witchcraft-for-real/

Webb Hodge, F. & Alexander, K. (n.d.). *Indian shamans & priests.* Legends of America. https://www.legendsofamerica.com/na-shaman/

What is the doll? (n.d.). Brown University. https://www.brown.edu/Departments/Joukowsky_Institute/courses/13things/7393.html

White, E. (2023, July 4). *Wicca.* Encyclopaedia Britannica. https://www.britannica.com/topic/Wicca

Wigington, P. (2018) *What is a Pagan Animal Familiar?* Learn Religions. learnreligions.com/what-is-an-animal-familiar-2562343

Women & the American Story. (n.d.). *Life story: Tituba.* https://wams.nyhistory.org/settler-colonialism-and-revolution/settler-colonialism/tituba/

Woodward, W. W. (2003). New England's Other Witch-Hunt: The Hartford Witch-Hunt of the 1660s and Changing Patterns in Witchcraft Prosecution. *OAH Magazine of History*, 17(4), 16–20. http://www.jstor.org/stable/25163616

Wright, R. (2004). The wicked and the wise men: witches and prophets in the history of the northwest Amazon. In: *In darkness and secrecy: the anthropology of assault sorcery and witchcraft in Amazonia.* Duke University Press. https://www.academia.edu/34023310

Zelenkoba, B. (2019, April 25). *Iemanja: A Uruguayan celebration of the Yoruba goddess of the sea.* The Ethnologist. https://ethnologist.info/2019/04/25/iemanja-a-uruguayan-celebration-of-the-yoruba-goddess-of-the-sea/

www.ingramcontent.com/pod-product-compliance
Lightning Source LLC
Chambersburg PA
CBHW051452130726
47987CB00005B/2282